Developing Managers
Through Behavior Modeling

Developing Managers Through Behavior Modeling

James C. Robinson

Developing Managers Through Behavior Modeling

Library of Congress Catalog Card Number: 82-81424
ISBN 0-89384-064-5
Printed in the United States of America

Learning Concepts
Austin, Texas

Distributed by
University Associates, Inc.
8517 Production Avenue
P.O. Box 26240
San Diego, California 92126

To Dana

Contents

Preface

Too Bad, Frank Sheppard!

Frank Sheppard had worked for the Dextron Manufacturing Corporation almost ten years before being promoted to supervisor of warehousing. Frank started with Dextron as an apprentice and worked his way up through a succession of more responsible jobs, finally to process operator. Even though his take-home pay would be about the same—because supervisors were not paid overtime—Frank took the promotion because he felt the position held even more opportunity for advancement.

Frank had been told that the warehouse supervisor's position was used to break in new supervisors. For the first ten months or so, Frank felt as though he was being smashed to pieces. Then things seemed to go a little easier. He had caught up with the paperwork, had a clearer picture of what a supervisor was supposed to do, and had even done a pretty good job of handling a couple of tough problems with employees.

After he had been on the job almost a year, Frank was notified that he had been enrolled in the DSDP—the Dextron Supervisory Development Program. Frank had heard a lot of good things about the DSDP: The people who had gone through it said it was interesting and enjoyable and gave them new ideas about how to supervise.

The DSDP was an eight-week program. Each week, the announcement said, fifteen supervisors would spend half a day studying a specific aspect of supervision. The first morning, Frank learned the eight sessions would cover the following aspects:

The Responsibilities of a Supervisor
Concepts of Motivation
Communicating with People
Problem Solving
Setting Objectives

Team Building

Developing People

Preparing an Action Plan

He was eager to get into it, especially to get some answers about motivating people and improving the productivity of his section.

Frank's initial enthusiasm grew stronger with each session. He agreed with many of the concepts presented and thought the case studies, some of which were on film, offered a lot of useful ideas. He especially enjoyed working with some of the other supervisors in small groups, discussing the different problems they had and developing "supervisory rules of thumb" for dealing with them. The instructor was very skillful. She listened to everyone's point of view and then summarized the key thoughts presented in the discussions.

In the eighth session, Frank developed an action plan for applying some of what he had learned about supervision. He outlined specific steps he would take to accomplish two objectives back on the job: (1) providing more recognition to employees who were doing satisfactory work and (2) increasing employees' involvement through mutual problem solving.

The day after Frank completed the action plan, he decided to start on his first objective by praising the work of Jack Sauer, one of his better employees. On his way to the cafeteria, Frank made it a point to stop by Jack's work area and say that he was really happy with Jack's performance, particularly his good housekeeping. Jack looked at Frank silently for a moment or two and then said, "If my performance is so good and my housekeeping is so great, when am I going to get a raise?" Frank, taken somewhat aback, stuttered, "Annual salary review. We'll talk about your salary at the annual review session. See you later, Jack." As he walked through the warehouse, Frank tried to remember what the DSDP had said about motivation and wondered why Jack had reacted the way he did. Frank also decided it would be a long, long time before he would stick his neck out to recognize any employee's performance.

The next week, Frank met with his boss, Chris Mahoney, for a routine review of warehousing operations. He mentioned he had enjoyed the eight weeks of DSDP and told Chris that one of the objectives of his action plan was to start doing mutual problem solving with employees. Chris sat quietly as Frank outlined his approach and then said, "Listen, Frank, I know that you want to be a good supervisor, and I think you will be—one of these days. But let me tell you something about what you learned in that course. A lot of those things just don't work in a company like ours. Take this mutual problem solving, for example. Frank, it takes a lot more time to solve problems when you try to involve eleven employees. And, Frank, you'll never get the employees to agree with you on anything. My advice to you is to forget the mutual problem solving. You're being paid to solve problems and make decisions, so why don't you do it that way?''

Frank decided to supervise the warehousing section the way he had been doing it before going to DSDP.

Unfortunately, Frank Sheppard's situation is not unusual. It happens every day in business, commerce, and government. When supervisors and managers learn concepts of management but do not learn the skills needed to apply them with employees, there is very little chance that they will be able to use those concepts with success. When their learning from the classroom is not reinforced by their superiors, there is very little chance they will use that learning on the job.

And that's why this book was written—to illustrate how the use of behavior modeling can lead to management-development programs in which people *will* develop skills and then *use* those skills on the job.

Introduction

The Effectiveness of Management Development and Other Myths

If you could assemble four generations of training-and-development professionals in one room and ask them how to approach management development—to improve or increase the performance of management and supervisors—their answers would chart the uncertain course of management development over the last thirty years. You would hear about a relatively unsystematic assortment of content concerns, instructional strategies, and methods, the combination of which has produced rather uncertain results—until the emergence in the early Seventies of a promising teaching-learning methodology known as behavior modeling.

Ask the Fifties' generation first. Most likely they would answer, "Managers and supervisors need to understand the functions of management, like planning, organizing, directing, coordinating, and controlling." The more progressive contingent of that generation would mention management by objectives. As for methods, they would talk about lectures, question-and-answer periods, and sometimes audiovisual presentations. The avant-garde of the Fifties would point with pride to their use of case studies or the laboratory method. The Sixties' group would emphasize the need for managers to be more concerned about human relations and to be more participative in their management approach. They would describe the addition of participative-learning techniques in their repertoire of methods—role plays, simulations, and business games. The group from the Seventies would point to the need for managers and supervisors to be able to deal with new issues rising from accelerated social and technological change—such as minorities and women in the work force, how to deal with the values of "the new worker," and appropriate organizational responses to mounting governmental regulation. They would point to their advances in the use of experiential learning, with a major emphasis on increasing managers' awareness. Some would talk in terms of competency-based learning—less theory, more practice. And you would hear the term *behavior modeling* mentioned for the first time.

Management development has evolved and grown to the point that more time, effort, and resources are being expended on it today than thirty years ago. Unfortunately, for most organizations, the return on the investment of greater resources has been less than satisfactory. In the eyes of the dispassionate, objective line manager, the results of management development have—at best—been varied; at worst, a waste of time and resources. The impartial top manager's assessment would be that management development has produced more failures than successes. The bottom line is that management development has not had nearly the impact on organizations that it should have had.

SOME SUCCESS STORIES

Behavior modeling is an approach to management development that works, that has been proven to have major, demonstrable impacts on the organization. The focus of the behavior-modeling approach is to change *behaviors*, rather than to transfer knowledge or change attitudes. Reduced to its bare essence, behavior modeling involves learning by watching and practicing. The learner acquires the target behaviors by watching a "model" demonstrate them on film or videotape, then reproduces those behaviors in an intensive guided practice.[1]

From the first time behavior-modeling techniques were applied for training supervisors, behavior modeling has accounted for some of the bright spots, some of the dramatic success stories, in the history of management development. Just through the Seventies, more than five hundred organizations world-wide had used behavior modeling to train their managers and supervisors. The results in these organizations—and the growing body of research on the efficacy of behavior modeling— have shown that when behavior modeling is correctly applied and implemented effectively, it can improve managerial skills and increase managers' effectiveness.

---

[1]As with any new technology, behavior modeling has given rise to a jargon among its practitioners. This book uses some of the most commonly accepted terms to convey the precise meanings or special connotations required in any discussion of behavior modeling: *Model, modeling display,* and *skill-practice exercise* are a few examples. For those who are not familiar with the subject, a short glossary is provided at the end of this book.

Here are three short examples from behavior modeling's early history.

General Electric (GE)

In 1970, management at the GE jet-engine plant in Evendale, Ohio, had begun an aggressive recruitment program to bring minorities into its work force. A good number of minority workers were hired, but to GE's dismay, over 70 percent left the organization after six months. The solution to this problem was a training program to help new employees adapt to and cope with a job in industry. New employees and their supervisors were trained in separate but parallel sessions on how to give and receive constructive criticism, how to ask for and give help, and how to establish mutual trust and respect. The training approach used with both groups was behavior modeling. As a result, 72 percent of the trained employees remained on the job more than six months (Burnaska, 1976). The impact on the organization was substantially reduced recruitment and selection costs and a commitment to increased minority employment.

American Telephone & Telegraph (AT&T)

In the early Seventies, AT&T management was concerned about the way supervisors would deal with changes in its work force. Management realized that many jobs (e.g., the position of telephone operator) that had traditionally been staffed by females would in the future be filled by a significant number of males—and vice versa. Management was also concerned that supervisors might not be able to deal effectively with the increasing number of minorities employed by AT&T.

The management tested and eventually selected the behavior-modeling approach to enable line supervisors to interact more effectively with their subordinates. In addition to building skills around typical supervisory concerns—such as improving the quality and quantity of work, reducing absenteeism, and conducting performance appraisals— the program enabled supervisors to handle complaints of discrimination, cases of insubordination, and employee resistance to supervision that might stem from differences in race or sex.

To evaluate the effectiveness of the program, ninety trained supervisors and ninety-three untrained supervisors were observed in simulated supervisory situations. The situations were handled exceptionally well or above average by 84 percent of the trained supervisors, compared to only 33 percent of the untrained supervisors. Only 6 percent of the trained supervisors handled the situations unsatisfactorily versus 33 percent of the untrained supervisors (Moses & Ritchie, 1976). After follow-up studies demonstrated that supervisors continued to use the skills on the job, AT&T implemented the program throughout the Bell System to train tens of thousands of supervisors. The program was considered a major factor in enabling AT&T to weather a period during which its work force was dramatically changing.

International Business Machines (IBM)

The IBM management was concerned about employee morale in its branch offices. The trial solution, a behavior-modeling-based program, was implemented in eighteen branches. The assumption was that if managers could communicate more effectively with employees, morale would improve. The training program emphasized learning how to provide feedback on opinion-survey information and how to prepare meaningful action plans to improve morale.

Back on the job, the performance of the eighteen trained branch managers was compared with a control group of thirteen untrained branch managers. Of the employees supervised by the trained managers, 31 percent had a more favorable opinion after opinion-survey feedback, versus only 20 percent supervised by the control group. Also, they had significantly more favorable impressions of the following: the company, IBM's earnings versus other companies', the amount of work, the manager, and advancement opportunities. Their overall satisfaction was 10 percent higher than the control group's employees' (Smith, 1976). Because of the favorable results, IBM expanded its skill training that used behavior modeling to other managers as well as to other skill areas, such as customer service and sales.

FROM PREVIEW TO PROMISE

These early applications at GE, AT&T, and IBM are but a preview of what behavior modeling can be expected to accomplish.

The rest of this book describes and illustrates in detail what behavior modeling is, how it is used, what it can be expected to accomplish, and why it works. As you will see, the focus is on managerial behavior, to demonstrate how behavior modeling can be used to enhance a wide range of management skills. In its broadest sense, the book speaks to anyone who has a stake in management development—anyone who wants to see supervisors and managers improve their skills, to see the skills learned in the classroom actually used on the job, or to receive a positive return on the resources invested in the training of managers and supervisors.

The main objectives of this book are the following:

1. To describe the learning theory and rationale supporting the use of behavior modeling techniques in management development.
2. To describe when and when not to use behavior modeling.
3. To describe how to design a behavior-modeling-based program and how to develop and use the required software.
4. To examine the organizational systems and implementation issues around the use of behavior-modeling programs.
5. To examine methods of evaluating a behavior-modeling program and to summarize what the research indicates about the effectiveness of behavior modeling to date.

As a whole, the chapters to come speak to training professionals and line managers who are interested in learning about the value and potential applications of behavior modeling in management development. However, the practical considerations in the development, implementation, and evaluation of successful behavior-modeling programs are surveyed from the standpoint of three distinct roles within the training function: the training manager, the program developer, and the classroom instructor. The expectation is that training managers will use the book as an orientation to the requirements associated with each role, with the chapters concerning decision making and overall program design speaking most directly to their personal role. Program-development staff and instructors, on the other hand, will find the particulars of their roles emphasized in the chapters concerning software development and procedures for using it. Although the focus of this book is the use of behavior modeling in management development, readers concerned with other applications should have no trouble translating the general process and techniques to customer contact, sales, and other training situations.

Chapters 1 and 2 will tell you why behavior modeling is effective, what makes it work, and when and when not to use it. Chapters 3 through 5 move into program-development concerns. You will find out how to determine and specify effective managerial behaviors, how to create modeling displays, and how to develop skill-practice exercises. Chapters 6 and 7 emphasize instructional procedures. They explore how to make the most of a modeling display in the classroom and how to use skill-practice exercises to develop skills and self-confidence.

Chapters 8 and 9 move back into broader program-implementation concerns. You will read about the power of management reinforcement and how it can make the difference between a successful and unsuccessful implementation of a behavior-modeling program. You will also learn what you can do to obtain management support for a behavior-modeling program. Chapter 10 deals with the program evaluation from the standpoint of management.

Chapter 11 deals with what the research indicates about the efficacy of behavior modeling. From this chapter, you will be able to draw conclusions that will help you plan how to use behavior modeling in management-development programs. The concluding chapter forecasts the use of behavior modeling in its second decade.

A book can provide only a road map and guidelines. This book cannot provide the skills needed to develop the modeling displays and skill-practice exercises for a behavior-modeling program, nor can it provide skills to conduct classroom sessions or to gain management support. The goal of this book is to provide sufficient knowledge to make an informed decision about whether behavior modeling is an appropriate technology for a given training situation. Lengthy case examples have been used to show concrete details of the manner in which some specific behavior-modeling techniques can be implemented and to illustrate what is needed to make them work. My hope is that the book will at least be useful in introducing you to behavior modeling and its uses.

REFERENCES

Burnaska, R.F. The effects of modeling training upon managers' behaviors and employees' perceptions. *Personnel Psychology*, 1976, *29*(3), 329-335.

Moses, J.L., & Ritchie, R.J. Supervisory relationships training: A behavioral evaluation of a behavior modeling program. *Personnel Psychology*, 1976, *29*(3), 337-343.

Smith, P.E. Management modeling training to improve morale and customer satisfaction. *Personnel Psychology*, 1976, *29*(3), 351-359.

1

What Makes Behavior Modeling Work? The Conceptual Framework

The use of behavior modeling in management development began humbly enough at General Electric in 1970, with the training of a handful of supervisors. No more than a dozen management-development applications of behavior modeling had occurred by 1974. With the advent of proprietary behavior-modeling programs in the mid-Seventies, more and more organizations began using the technology through the second half of the decade. By the beginning of 1980, approximately one million employees in both the private and public sectors had been trained with the aid of behavior-modeling programs.

The primary reason for the tremendous growth of the use of behavior modeling is that it works. It provides learners with skills that make them more effective on the job. The question, then, is, *"What makes it work?"*

This chapter explains and illustrates what principles behavior modeling has drawn from our knowledge of adult learning and how they are translated into a behavior-modeling program. It forms an overview of the main program-development tasks and instructional procedures required for successful behavior-modeling programs—requirements that are explored more fully in subsequent chapters.

THE UNDERLYING PRINCIPLES

Behavior modeling is effective because it is based on sound learning theory. It represents a back-to-the-basics, straightforward approach to learning—no chrome, no mag wheels, no fluff. It is simply an effective, efficient framework and process for learning.

The behavior-modeling approach is founded on four research-based principles of adult learning: modeling or imitation, behavioral rehearsal or practice, reinforcement or reward, and transfer.[2] In brief, learning via behavior modeling requires imitation of effective behaviors, intensive guided practice in the performance of new behaviors, and reinforcement or recognition for the learner's demonstration and application of the new behaviors. In management development, as well as in other applications, the focus of behavior modeling is on changing *behaviors*—specific managerial behaviors, usually those required in problematic situations involving interaction with one or more employees—rather than on transferring knowledge or shaping attitudes.

Rehearsal, reinforcement, and transfer are familiar concepts for training professionals working in the realm of management development. What may be unfamiliar, in practice at any rate, is the notion of modeling, which has a long history in psychological research and has been examined under many other labels, e.g., observational or vicarious learning. It is an integral concept in social-learning theory, which holds that we learn a great deal of our behavior by watching others and remembering both what they did and the outcomes of their behaviors. The social-learning theorists distinguish between acquisition (learning) and reproduction (performance). Modeling is the vehicle for acquisition. Conditioning principles, with heavy emphasis on social reinforcers, tend to account for performance. For a deeper understanding of modeling in the context of social-learning theory, consult Bandura (1971).

Although the use of modeling has a long history in technical training, it was not until Goldstein and Sorcher (1974) worked with GE in the early Seventies that it was applied to train others in complex interpersonal-communication tasks. Zemke (1978) makes the point succinctly:

> Anyone who has tried to write or even read repair instructions for anything more complex than a rubber band appreciates modeling and learning by imitation. In technical training, the score has always been: talk about it = 0, see diagrams of it = 10; watch someone do it = 1,000 (p. 23).

The good news from the early work with behavior modeling at GE, AT&T, IBM, and Agway was that certain managerial skills could be learned effectively via modeling in combination with the use of rehearsal, reinforcement, and transfer principles (Burnaska, 1976; Byham & Robinson, 1976; Goldstein & Sorcher, 1974; Moses & Ritchie, 1976; Smith, 1976).

---

[2]Goldstein and Sorcher (1974) describe the four principles (albeit using slightly different labels) and offer examples of how they operationalized them in their early implementations of behavior modeling. They offer a comprehensive investigation of the empirical basis of the behavior-modeling approach. For an overview of the theory behind behavior modeling, see Zemke (1978).

In essence, the modeling aspect of behavior modeling involves presenting to a group of learners, on film or videotape, the behaviors necessary to accomplish a specific outcome. In management-development applications, the outcome is most frequently the successful resolution of a particular supervisor-subordinate problem—for example, taking disciplinary action for a work-rule infraction or handling an employee complaint. Then skill practice, or behavioral rehearsal, comes into play. The learners are provided with extended structured opportunities and encouragement to practice the behaviors demonstrated by the model. Reinforcement occurs immediately via instructor-managed feedback on each learner's performance in successive skill practices. On-the-job reinforcement is accomplished by various means, frequently by training the learners' superiors in reinforcement skills.

FIVE PRECEPTS

Various proponents of behavior modeling may emphasize one aspect of the behavior-modeling approach over another or use different terms to label them; different practitioners certainly employ different specifics (e.g., videotaping the skill practices). Nevertheless, in current practice, the underlying principles of behavior modeling can be translated into five precepts governing the design and conduct of behavior-modeling-based programs for management development: *behavioral objectives, model, skill practice, immediate feedback,* and *on-the-job reinforcement.* Each points to a necessary but dependent component of the behavior-modeling approach. Figure 1 illustrates their derivation from the adult-learning principles described earlier and specifies some of the program-development and classroom-instruction concerns they generate. As mentioned in later chapters, the need to adhere to these precepts carries through from overall program design to software development, classroom instruction, and transfer to the job.

Behavioral Objectives

If you can't describe it in behavioral terms, don't try to teach it.

This is the first precept of behavior modeling. The intended outcomes of the learning experience must be expressed in behavioral terms.

For purposes of program development—and from the standpoint of overall program success—the behavioral objectives must meet two criteria: (1) They must be based on the needs of the learner, and (2) they must specify *effective* behavior. When behavioral objectives are based on the real needs of the learner, he or she will readily see the benefits that can be derived from learning the target skills. When the objectives specify behavior that will increase the learner's effectiveness on the job, the learner receives an immediate payoff when he or she first uses the skills back at the work place.

LEARNING PRINCIPLES	BEHAVIOR-MODELING PRECEPTS	PROGRAM-DEVELOPMENT CONSIDERATIONS	CLASSROOM PROCEDURES
Modeling	*Behavioral Objectives* If you can't describe it in behavioral terms, don't try to teach it.	Define behavioral objectives that • Are based on needs. • Specify *effective* behavior.	1. Introduce need for skill.
			2. Present critical steps.
	Model If you can't demonstrate how to do it, don't teach it.	Develop modeling displays that • Are positive. • Are credible.	3. Show modeling display.
Behavioral Rehearsal	*Skill Practice* If you can't practice the skill, you can't develop it.	Develop skill-practice exercises that • Provide each learner extended opportunities to perform the behaviors. • Provide success experiences.	4. Review critical steps. 5. Provide skill practices for learners.
Reinforcement	*Immediate Feedback* Without feedback there's no accurate basis for changing some behaviors and strengthening others.	Develop instructor competencies for managing feedback process that • Reinforce effective behaviors. • Provide alternative behaviors.	6. Manage process of group feedback on the learners' performances after each skill practice.
Transfer	*On-the-job Reinforcement* Without reinforcement on the job, the new skills will be extinguished.	Arrange for separate management-reinforcement workshops for learners' immediate superiors.	

Figure 1.
Behavior Modeling: The Conceptual Framework in Management Development

To meet the first criterion, a needs analysis should be conducted to determine what skills the learners must possess to handle their specific jobs effectively. *Skill area* refers to a broad category of job-related behaviors that will enable the learner to handle a specific situation effectively (e.g., routine complaints from subordinates). The needs analysis also provides data about the target learners' current skill levels in each area. Once the skill levels are identified, the appropriate skill areas for training can be selected.

As for the second criterion, the behavioral objectives must *specify* behaviors that will enable the learners to handle their jobs in real life effectively. For example, if a salesperson needs to learn how to handle a customer complaint, the behavioral objectives must specify a set of effective behaviors that would—when used by a salesperson—satisfactorily resolve a customer complaint.

Behavioral objectives are shared with the learners so they will know what they are expected to achieve in each *skill module* (i.e., a classroom session devoted to learning behaviors in a given skill area). The behavioral objectives are presented to the learners as a set of *critical steps*, a succinct check list of behaviors. For example, the critical steps for handling routine complaints from employees might be the following:

1. Listen intently and respond with empathy to the employee.
2. Obtain all the details of the complaint and make notes.
3. Respond by showing that you understand the situation.
4. Openly present your position.
5. Decide on specific action and a follow-up date.
6. Thank the employee for bringing the complaint to your attention.

The critical steps guide the learner through the demonstration and the skill-practice segments of the module and, later, are used as a check list in handling the situation on the job.

Model

If you can't demonstrate how to do it, don't teach it.

The second precept of behavior modeling requires a demonstration of the effective use of the behaviors. In current practice, this demonstration occurs via a filmed or videotaped vignette.

The term *model* is used to refer to the person handling a particular situation in the filmed or taped vignette. *The model demonstrates the behavior that the learner should learn to use.* The term *modeling display* refers to the entire vignette in which a model handles a specific situation by using the skills that the participants are learning.

The model must seem *positive* and *credible* to the learners. To be positive, a model must demonstrate behaviors that are effective for a given situation. Ineffective or irrelevant behaviors should not be included in the modeling display. When the modeling display shows only positive behavior, the learners will not be distracted by demonstrations and discussions of methods that should not be used. To be credible, the model must be perceived by the learners as competent and effective and the situation must seem true to life. A positive, credible modeling display shows the learners a way of handling situations they can identify with and learn from.

For example, if sales representatives are learning the skill of overcoming objections, the modeling display should show a model sales representative who is successfully overcoming objections from a potential customer. The model must appear effective and the potential customer must appear real. The objections raised by the would-be customer must be similar to those normally heard by the learners. Under these conditions, the learners will identify with the model and the skill demonstrated in the modeling display. They will feel they *can* learn the new skill, and they will *want* to learn the behaviors because they will recognize them as being effective in a real-life sales situation.

Skill Practice

If you can't practice the skill, you can't develop it.

A *skill practice*[3] is an instructor-managed exercise in which one learner practices the behaviors previously demonstrated by the model. The purpose of the skill practices is to provide each learner with numerous opportunities to enact the critical steps by recalling and performing the behaviors used by the model.

An effective skill practice gives the learner a success experience, both in early trials and later on, as the situations become more complex. A skill practice is a success experience only when learners develop both skill *and* confidence. Developing only skill or only confidence is not enough.

---

[3]Although they are similar in concept, a *skill practice* differs from a *role play*, as that term is commonly used, because the exclusive purpose of a skill practice is the learner's demonstration of precise behavioral targets, whereas role plays can have a number of possible uses. A role-play activity, for example, may ask learners to produce their usual behaviors so their actions and resulting effectiveness can be analyzed, that is, the role play is commonly used to generate data, whereas the skill practice is strictly an "anticipatory rehearsal in the behaviors necessary to meet a given work-related problem" (Goldstein & Sorcher, 1974, p. 18).

To take an example from everyday life, a person may develop skills as a public speaker yet lack the confidence to speak effectively before large groups. Without confidence, the prospective public speaker will not use the skills in front of large groups, and vice versa. A person may have the confidence to make a presentation to a large group but lack the required skills—a potentially disastrous situation for speaker and audience alike.

The key to developing and conducting effective skill practices is to allow each learner numerous opportunities to practice the new behaviors and to feel successful in doing so.

Immediate Feedback

Without feedback there's no accurate basis for changing some behaviors and strengthening others.

After each skill practice, the learner must be given information about which behaviors that he or she used were effective and which were ineffective. With immediate feedback, the learner can appropriately modify specific behaviors until the skill is mastered. To be effective, the feedback must satisfy three criteria:

1. It must immediately follow the skill practice.
2. It must be expressed in a manner that reinforces the effective behaviors the learner demonstrated and must include an explanation of how and why the learner was effective in demonstrating the target behavior.
3. It must specify ways to be more effective and in what areas improvement is needed. The feedback must provide the learner with *alternative positive behaviors*, i.e., positive and effective alternatives, expressed in behavioral terms, for handling the situation in the future.

Effective immediate feedback reinforces effective behaviors *and* provides learners with alternative positive behaviors for the critical steps in which they could have been more effective. With effective feedback, the learners are able to modify their behaviors and perform better in their next opportunities to demonstrate the particular skill.

On-the-Job Reinforcement

Without reinforcement on the job, the new skills will be extinguished.

Management reinforcement is also vital to the success of a behavior-modeling-based program. Although in current practice various mechanisms are used to accomplish on-the-job reinforcement, the approach advocated in this book consists of management-reinforcement workshops for the learners' immediate superiors and management-support meetings involving higher management. The immediate superiors of the learners must be trained in how to reinforce the use of the newly learned skills on the job. Otherwise the learners may revert to their pretraining behavior. Management-support meetings are the recommended vehicle for overcoming obstacles to reinforcement that may be present within organizational systems and norms and for obtaining higher management's acceptance and endorsement of the skills the learners will transfer to the job.

The five precepts outlined above have evolved over more than a decade of experience in using behavior-modeling techniques. The following case example illustrates how some of those precepts influenced program development and classroom procedures in an early application of the behavior-modeling approach at Agway, Inc. The Agway story forms a part of the early history of the application of behavior-modeling techniques in management development—along with GE, IBM, and AT&T—and is representative of many of the early attempts. The example is intended not only to portray the state of the art in the early Seventies, but also to preview the design-and-implementation issues that are the concern of the rest of this book.

AN EXAMPLE: AGWAY INC.

Agway Inc. is a multi-billion-dollar farmers' cooperative that operates in twelve northeastern states. It is owned by 120,000 farmers and employs approximately fifteen thousand people.

In 1972, Agway was in the process of consolidating and relocating the operations of nine obsolete warehouses into three semiautomated distribution centers. The purpose of the consolidation and establishment of the new distribution centers was to increase the productivity of the distribution function.

The Agway management was concerned about merging the nine different work groups because some were union organized but most were not. It was Agway's intention to operate the new distribution centers on a union-free basis. Also, the Agway management was apprehensive that increased automation might eventually cause employee dissatisfaction and unrest. In addition, they were concerned that the values of the workers were changing and that the more assertive, independent worker would present problems that supervisors were not equipped to handle. They were fearful that this could result in work slowdowns or stoppages.

Management felt it must take a proactive role by establishing an open, supportive work environment—the kind that would minimize employee unrest. To verify their assessment, management asked Paul Steiger and me to conduct a situational analysis at the distribution center that began operation first—at Geneva, New York. Paul was personnel manager of the Physical Distribution Division, and I was the corporate training director.

The situational analysis conducted at Geneva revealed that supervisors were doing an adequate job of maintaining and directing the work flow. However, there were four provocative findings that pointed out important deficiencies in their skills, given management's concern about achieving the desired work environment and reducing potential dissatisfaction:

1. The employees viewed supervisors as inconsistent in their supervision. For example, employees said that on some days supervisors treated subordinates more harshly than they did on others.

2. Employees thought supervisors were not as responsive to employees' concerns and complaints as they should be. Employees said they believed supervisors did not care about their complaints.

3. Supervisors often performed tasks that could have been delegated to employees. Because the Geneva Distribution Center was nonunion, the supervisors were able to work along with employees whenever they wished. Employees often felt that the supervisors could use their time more effectively by concentrating on their supervisory responsibilities.

4. Supervisors were not as firm with some employees as they needed to be. They often avoided difficult situations with assertive subordinates.

Agway decided to train the warehouse supervisors in how to handle employee-performance discussions, deal with employee complaints, overcome resistance to change, and hold other types of discussions with employees. The approach selected was behavior modeling.

Program-Development Considerations

The situational analysis at Agway did not provide sufficient information for specifying behavioral objectives, so a follow-up series of patterned interviews with employees, supervisors, and managers identified the following specific areas in which skill development was needed:

1. Improving employee performance.
2. Discussing poor work habits.
3. Taking effective disciplinary action.
4. Providing recognition.
5. Handling employee complaints.
6. Delegating responsibility.
7. Motivating the average employee.
8. Teaching an employee a new job.
9. Overcoming resistance to change.

This list met the first criterion for developing behavioral objectives: It was based on needs, i.e., performance deficiencies. Improvement in these areas would enable the supervisors to overcome these deficiencies.

To meet the second criterion for behavioral objectives—specifying effective behavior—a precise set of behaviors had to be identified for each of the nine skills. The behaviors were defined through task analysis, direct observation, critical-incident analysis, and a review of the literature. They were then translated into the form of critical steps. For example, the critical steps for the skill "discussing poor work habits" are the following:

1. Indicate to the employee the behavior that you have observed.
2. Explain why it concerns you.
3. Ask the employee for reasons.
4. Indicate that the situation must change.
5. Discuss possible solutions.
6. Agree on specific activities and a follow-up date.

The purpose of the critical steps was to give supervisors a check list of the behaviors to be followed during training as well as back on the job when discussing poor work habits with deficient subordinates. The next step was the modeling displays.

Arnie Goldstein and Mel Sorcher, the pioneers in the use of behavior modeling for supervisory training, had produced their first modeling-display films in the summer of 1972. The skill areas determined as high priority needs at Geneva matched the content of the Goldstein and Sorcher films, but the settings were non-specific business environments. We were concerned about whether

Agway supervisors would be able to identify with a modeling display that did not use a warehouse setting.

We decided to use the Goldstein and Sorcher films on a trial basis to determine whether the model in the films would seem both positive and credible to the supervisors at the Geneva Distribution Center. We established three criteria for accepting the films for the training program:

1. The supervisors must perceive the situation as something that could have happened in real life.
2. They must perceive the model supervisor as effective in handling the situation in the film.
3. They must feel they could learn the skill being demonstrated.

In the pilot session, we asked six Geneva supervisors to comment on each modeling display, to determine how they perceived the film relative to the three criteria. Because they perceived seven of the nine films as positive and credible, we decided to use the films to train the other supervisors.

Classroom Procedures

During the sessions, each supervisor viewed the modeling display after a short introduction of the critical steps. After viewing the film, the supervisors and the instructor discussed behaviors that the model supervisor had used effectively in handling the situation. The supervisors were then expected to replicate them in the skill practices that followed.

To introduce the skill-practice segment of each module, we outlined a few situations similar to the modeling display that had occurred at the distribution centers. We then asked two supervisors to handle one of these situations as a skill practice. The supervisor who was given the subordinate's role in the skill practice was coached on how to approach the problem and how aggressively to pursue the subordinate's point of view. For example, for a skill practice involving "discussing poor work habits," we explained what the poor work habit was, what resistance to offer the supervisor, and what changes the supervisor should be willing to accept.

The supervisor in the skill practice was also coached about the situation and how to handle it. We coached the supervisor on how to follow the critical steps and what to do if the employee seemed cooperative or uncooperative. The supervisor was then asked to initiate the discussion with the subordinate about the poor work habit and to follow the critical steps in sequence.

Because the supervisors wanted to learn these skills and felt that they could, they tried to follow the critical steps and handle the discussions as effectively as possible. Coaching on the key issues and ways to handle potential problems helped the supervisors handle the skill-practice discussions successfully more than 80 percent of the time. When a supervisor could not handle the situation successfully, the skill practice was interrupted and the supervisor was coached on how to continue in a more productive vein.

During the skill practices, the instructor and the observers took notes on the dialog, which provided the basis for immediate feedback to the skill-practice supervisor. At the completion of each skill practice, the instructor asked the observers to focus their feedback on specific comments about behaviors that were particularly effective during the discussion. They were asked to describe the behavior and provide the reasons that the behavior was effective. For example, an observer might say, "Telling George that you were concerned about his personal safety was really effective, because it encouraged George to focus on himself rather than on the inconvenience of using the safety shield."

In addition, the observers were instructed to provide the supervisor with examples of behaviors used in the skill practice that were not effective. This feedback described the behavior, indicated the reasons it was not effective, and then provided the learner with an APB (alternative positive behavior). The following is a typical APB: "Instead of saying, 'You're just going to have to do it this way,' you could have been more effective if you had said, 'We both know that we have to get the job done, but we don't agree on how to do it. What suggestions do you have on how to do it?'"

Results

This application of behavior modeling enabled the supervisors at the Agway distribution centers to develop essential skills for effective supervision. To determine the effect of the training on the work climate—one of management's main concerns—a climate survey was conducted with employees at the Geneva Center just before the supervisors were trained and again three months after training. The surveys showed a 10-percent improvement in the work climate. The overall result of the program, and management's support for it, was that the three distribution centers were able to meet their productivity goals and function without work slowdowns or stoppages. Management considered the program so successful for the distribution function that it was extended to all of Agway's supervisors.

The principles and procedures making up the behavior-modeling approach to management development are not new, but not until 1970 were they systematically organized and applied to supervisory-skills training. Since then, evidence grows more conclusive that the use of behavior modeling brings about behavioral change in supervisory, worker, and other learner groups. The fundamental principles and procedures of the approach have been used with nonprofessional hospital staffs, law-enforcement and corrections officers, salespeople and customer-contact personnel, and numerous supervisors and managers. Its effectiveness as an instructional technology has been seen in a number of rigorous studies that indicate that training programs using behavior modeling result in the acquisition of specific skills, that the behaviors learned actually transfer to the job, and that they continue to be used effectively long after training.

The coming chapters explore some of the specific requirements for implementing behavior-modeling-based management-development programs and offer concrete procedures and techniques for a more thorough understanding of behavior modeling and its potential uses.

REFERENCES

Bandura, A. *Psychological modeling*. New York: Lieber-Atherton, 1971.

Burnaska, R.F. The effects of modeling training upon managers' behaviors and employees' perceptions. *Personnel Psychology*, 1976, *29*(3), 329-335.

Byham, W.C., & Robinson, J.C. Interaction modeling: A new concept in supervisory training. *Training and Development Journal*, 1976, *30*(2), 20-23.

Goldstein, A., & Sorcher, M. *Changing supervisor behavior*. Elmsford, NY: Pergamon Press, 1974.

Moses, J.L., & Ritchie, R.J. Supervisory relationships training: A behavioral evaluation of a behavior modeling program. *Personnel Psychology*, 1976, *29*(3), 337-343.

Smith, P.E. Management modeling training to improve morale and customer satisfaction. *Personnel Psychology*, 1976, *29*(3), 351-359.

Zemke, R. Behavior modeling: Using the "monkey see, monkey do" principle in training. *Training*, 1978, *15*(6), 21-26.

2

Making a Decision: To Use or Not To Use Behavior Modeling

Behavior modeling works—when it is well designed and well implemented and when it is the appropriate technology for the training situation. Although later chapters deal with how to design and implement behavior-modeling programs, this chapter deals with how to decide whether or not behavior modeling is the appropriate technology for a given training situation.

Consider some typical training situations. For which ones would behavior modeling be an appropriate technology? For which ones would it not?

- Sales representatives need to diagnose the specific needs of a potential customer.
- Supervisors need to increase their awareness of male/female interactions.
- Airline service representatives need to handle overbooked-flight situations with passengers.
- Managers need to become aware of how their management styles impact others.

To determine whether behavior modeling is an appropriate approach, you must ask the right questions, obtain accurate information, and make sound decisions.

SEVEN QUESTIONS TO ASK

Seven major questions should be asked when deciding whether or not to use behavior modeling. The questions are shown as a flow chart in Figure 2 to illustrate the sequence of the seven decision points necessary to determine whether behavior-modeling technology is appropriate for a given situation. For example, if an opinion survey shows that most employees feel that the performance appraisals conducted by their

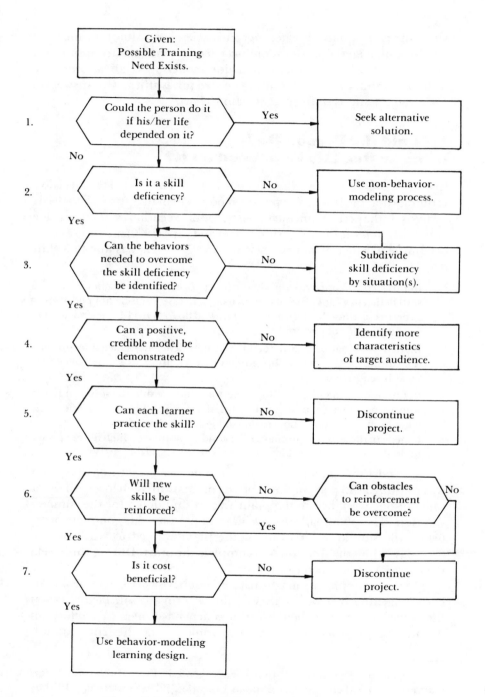

Figure 2. Behavior-Modeling Decision Flow Chart

supervisors are unfair, threatening, and useless, a possible training need would be managerial skills to conduct effective performance appraisals. Determining whether or not behavior modeling is an appropriate technology to apply to that training need requires affirmative answers to the seven questions in the decision flow chart.

1. Could the Person Do It If His or Her Life Depended on It?

In other words, is it a *training* problem or not? The crux of this decision is the one that the Praxis Corporation points to in its approach to needs analysis: Is the performance deficiency one of execution or of knowledge (and skill)? It is the same decision Mager and Pipe (1970) mention as they determine whether or not the performance deficiency is due to a skill deficiency.

> In this step you must decide whether the performance deficiency is due to a skill deficiency (or knowledge deficiency). In essence, is he not performing as desired because he does not know how to do it? If his life depended on it, would he still not perform?
>
> If there is a genuine skill (or knowledge) deficiency, then the primary remedy must either change his skill level (teach him how to do it) or change what is required of him.
>
> If, on the other hand, he is able to perform but doesn't, the solution lies in something other than enhancing his skills. "Teaching" someone to do what he already knows how to do isn't going to change his skill level. The remedy in these cases is to change the conditions under which he is expected to do that which he already knows how to do. (p. 17)[4]

Consider this example: The rework rate on a machining operation was running at 13 percent but dropped dramatically when a rush order came in one week before the plant was to shut down for the summer vacation. The plant had just five days to produce this complete order before the shutdown. No one in the plant wanted to work on the Saturday before the shutdown to complete the order. During this week, the rework rate dropped to 5 percent.

In this example, the machinists did not have a deficiency of skill or knowledge. In other words, they could perform at a satisfactory rate if their lives (or at least their vacations) depended on it. Therefore, in diagnosing this situation, the answer would be that they could do it if

---

[4]Reprinted by permission from R.F. Mager & P. Pipe. *Analyzing Performance Problems*. Belmont, CA: Pitman Learning, 1970. Copyright © 1970 by Pitman Learning, Inc.

their lives depended on it. Because it was not a deficiency of skill or knowledge, the organization needed to find an alternate solution to the rework problem.

2. Is It a Skill Deficiency?

Determine whether the performance deficiency is due to a deficiency of skill or a deficiency of knowledge. Although the intended results of a training program are frequently the acquisition of both skill and knowledge, the appropriate learning experiences for gaining a skill are different from those for gaining knowledge.

Consider this example: In a program designed to teach student pilots to fly aircraft, the learners have to acquire both knowledge and skill. They need to understand the theory of flying to know why an aircraft leaves the ground at certain speeds, why the spoilers on the wings of an aircraft are used to reduce lift on landing, what effect a thunderstorm has on flight characteristics, and so on. Learning these facts would require knowledge acquisition. At the same time, they must develop certain skills to perform certain tasks. For example, they have to learn how to push the throttle forward for power during takeoff, how to control the rudders with their feet, how to control the ailerons and elevators with their hands, and how to read the instruments. Learning these things requires skill development.

Although behavior modeling would not be appropriate for teaching the theory of flight, it could be considered for teaching new pilots the skills needed to control the aircraft.

3. Can the Behaviors Needed To Overcome the Skill Deficiency Be Identified?

Teaching a person to pilot an aircraft requires identifying the skills needed for each maneuver. In examining the skills required for aircraft takeoff, the instructor can identify specific behaviors a pilot must use when the plane is lined up on the runway ready for takeoff: a specific hand movement to increase the power to the throttles, specific methods for controlling the rudders to keep the aircraft down the center on the runway, a specific time that the yoke must be pulled back to raise the nose of the aircraft, and a specific pattern in which the pilot's eyes must follow the gauges to assure constant speed. These are *general* behaviors that can be identified for the pilot of any aircraft. Nevertheless, pilot behaviors differ considerably from one type of aircraft to another. In a 747, for example, the behaviors would be more complex, require interaction with other members of the flight crew, and require a different set of decision rules (e.g., the speed at which the nose wheel lifts off the ground).

When developing a behavior-modeling program, you will often find that you have identified *general* behaviors when you really need behaviors *specific* to an individual situation. To identify specific behaviors, you must study each situation. In the airplane analogy, the instructor must identify the behaviors for the specific type of aircraft.

In another example, consider a salesperson's inability to build rapport with new clients. You may find that one set of behaviors is not sufficient to cover all situations. There may be various types of clients, each of whom requires a different set of behaviors. For example, clients may be categorized as quiet, openly hostile, having a specific problem and needing help in analyzing that problem, or having already decided on the type of equipment wanted and its specifications.

The first general rule for making the decision to identify more behaviors is "Behaviors do not have to be identified by situation if the required behaviors are very similar in several different situations." The second general rule is "The behaviors for each situation must be identified separately if a specific behavior is a make-or-break behavior [such as landing a specific type of aircraft] and if this behavior is not generally displayed in other situations."

4. Can a Positive, Credible Model Be Demonstrated?

Two issues are involved in this decision. First, can a *positive* model be demonstrated? That is, can you present those behaviors required for the learner to handle that situation effectively on the job? (Methods for determining the behavioral objectives and testing their effectiveness are discussed in Chapter 3.)

If effective behaviors can be identified, the second issue is whether or not learners will perceive the model as *credible*. They will perceive the model as credible only when they can answer yes to three questions.

1. Could the situation I just viewed have happened in real life?
2. Did the model handle the situation effectively?
3. Could I learn to do the same thing?

If the answer to the first question is no, the situation in the modeling display seems artificial to the audience and additional characteristics of the target audience should be identified. Imagine a mining operation with tremendous noise. Supervisors there could not relate to a model supervisor in a quiet office setting. A modeling display in which the model supervisor would be depicted in a noisy environment—not an office—would need to be developed.

If the answer to the second question is no, the behaviors of the model differ too much from the norms of the organization to be accepted by the learners. Again, more characteristics of the target audience, including its perception of organizational norms, must be identified. Once this is done, a credible model can most likely be developed.

If the answer to the third question is no, the skills of the model are so sophisticated that the learners do not see themselves becoming that skillful. For this reason, it is imperative that the model demonstrate a *satisfactory* skill level rather than exceptional skill.

An example of the importance of demonstrating an appropriate skill level in the modeling display would be a situation in which supervisors were not skillful in taking disciplinary action. These supervisors would probably have tremendous anxiety in the classroom, because disciplinary action is a very important supervisory responsibility and because they would not have been handling it well. Therefore, the model should portray a supervisor with satisfactory—but not exceptional—skills. Otherwise, the supervisors would not be likely to see the model's behavior as something they could learn.

5. Can Each Learner Practice the Skill?

Decision 5 boils down to whether or not the organization can afford to provide each learner an opportunity for skill practice. It is normally a question of whether or not it is *cost beneficial* to provide each learner with such an opportunity.

For instance, suppose someone advocated that all airline passengers on over-water flights practice using flotation equipment in a water tank or swimming pool to ensure that everyone could float with the flotation device when fully clothed. If a passenger could not do that, he or she would be provided with coaching and feedback on how to use the flotation equipment in a safe manner.

Although it is *possible* to provide every passenger on an over-water flight with this skill practice, the practical considerations are too great. It would require, for example, that passengers arrive at the airport early, and some provision for changing and drying out their clothes would have to be made. Tanks of water would have to be installed, and lifeguards would have to be hired to ensure passenger safety. It would be a costly skill practice, and the costs would outweigh the benefits.

Therefore, in Decision 5, the paramount issue is whether or not the benefits of skill practice outweigh the costs.

6. Will the New Skills Be Reinforced?

Decision 6 concerns *reinforcement* both within and outside the classroom. Classroom reinforcement is easy to achieve. Instructors can learn to handle the group dynamics to gain social reinforcement within the class. If the needs analysis is carefully done and the group dynamics of the class are handled well, reinforcement will follow as the participants practice the skills and receive feedback on the use of those skills.

On-the-job reinforcement, however, is often much more difficult to achieve. At this decision point, a thorough analysis must be made to determine whether or not there will be sufficient reinforcement for sustained use of the new skills on the job. Although it is impractical in this book to list every possible reinforcement, the following are four of the most important categories to consider in the analysis.

Self-Reinforcement. In looking at self-reinforcement, analyze whether or not the new skills will provide the learner with a perceived payoff and whether or not those skills are compatible with the learner's value system.

When supervisors learn the skill "overcoming resistance to change," they will most likely see that employees are more receptive to change when their supervisors introduce it skillfully. However, the supervisors also discover that they must involve subordinates in the decision-making process. If this method conflicts with their beliefs about what a supervisor should do, they may elect not to use the skill. Therefore, in determining whether or not a newly learned skill is self-reinforcing, look closely at the values of the target learners and the environment in which they operate.

Peer Reinforcement. Peers are also a potential source of reinforcement. The general rule is "The greater the number of one's co-workers who use the skill, the more peer reinforcement that person will receive."

For example, suppose a supervisor has difficulty accepting the value of involving subordinates in the change process. He or she has been and is now—even after training—more comfortable in making all decisions without employee involvement. If this supervisor sees that many peer supervisors are successfully involving their subordinates in the change process, the supervisor may question the reluctance to use the skill and decide it is worth a try.

Management Reinforcement. Managers, of course, are a crucial source of reinforcement. (This entire issue is treated more completely in Chapter 8.) In all cases, the learner's immediate supervisor is a most powerful reinforcer.

Here is a preview of how a manager can provide reinforcement as a coach, as a reinforcer, and as a model.

- *As a Coach.* In assuming the role of coach, the manager provides subordinates with help in determining what skills to use in a given situation and then how to implement those skills. For example, as a coach, the district sales manager might help a sales representative diagnose what skills to use with a customer who is openly hostile and provide coaching on how to handle the customer.

- *As a Reinforcer.* To act as a reinforcer, the manager provides recognition and praise when the subordinate uses the newly learned skills. Shortly after classroom training, it is important that the learner try to use the new skills on the job and that the manager provide the individual with reinforcement and recognition. For example, shortly after training, a supervisor tries a new skill of delegation. The supervisor delegates weekly safety inspections and reports to a key employee. The supervisor's manager should observe what is happening, that is, whether or not the supervisor is using the new delegation skill. Then the manager should give the supervisor praise for delegating the safety inspection and report. This praise will encourage the supervisor to do even more delegating in the future.

- *As a Model.* In the classroom, the model is an important element in the learning experience. Likewise, a positive model on the job is crucial to the ongoing use of the skills. Because a person's immediate supervisor is usually the most credible model, one way to increase the ongoing use of the new skills is to make sure that the individual's manager is a positive on-the-job model for those skills.

Organization Reinforcement. Still another source of reinforcement to consider is reinforcement by the organization itself. Many times the organization does not reinforce the use of newly learned skills. The main task at this decision point is to examine the reward-and-punishment system. Unfortunately, many organizations do not reward the use of newly learned skills. In fact, sometimes the organization actually punishes those who practice them. For example, it may be unprofitable for a salesperson to handle a customer complaint effectively because the time lost could have been used to make commissions on sales.

When an analysis indicates that there are organizational obstacles to reinforcement, each barrier should be diagnosed. Once identified, each obstacle must be analyzed to determine whether or not it can be overcome.

Here is an actual case. An organization was considering supervisory-skills training for line supervisors in a diesel-engine assembly plant. The supervisory-skills program would enable them to interact more effectively with employees when discussing performance problems, handling employee complaints, introducing change, delegating responsibility, and fulfilling other major supervisory functions. However, the needs analysis indicated that supervisors' performance ratings were heavily influenced by the quality control department's report on each assembled engine. Because a high defect rate had the punishing effect of lowering the performance rating, each supervisor worked on each engine to eliminate any defects. Thus the supervisors were encouraged to become "working" supervisors rather than "managing" supervisors. This barrier could have been overcome by changing the reward system so that it was as rewarding for supervisors to spend time supervising people as checking out defects in the final product.

7. Is It Cost Beneficial?

Will there be a positive return on the investment for the training? To determine this, use the following formula:

$$\frac{\text{Value of Training}}{\text{Cost of Training}} = \text{Return on Investment}$$

The *value of training* is determined by computing the dollar value of correcting a performance deficiency, preventing a problem from occurring, or maximizing an opportunity. Examples of performance deficiencies would be poor product quality, poor client relations, or the inability to develop reliable budgets. In preventing a problem from occurring, the value of training could center around providing managers with the skills of monitoring their operations so that problems will be nipped in the bud. Training for the ability to develop new markets would fall in the category of maximizing opportunities.

The first step is to establish the dollar value of correcting the deficiency, preventing the problem, or maximizing the opportunity. This, of course, is related to the original training need, which began the decision-making process. Granted, the original training need may now have been changed and redefined through the analysis. Its redefinition, however, probably has helped determine even more precisely the value of the training.

To calculate the *cost of training*, add the costs of the following items:

- Front-end analysis.
- Development or purchase of training materials.
- Salaries of participants while in the classroom.
- Salaries of instructors while in the classroom.
- Breaking down the barriers to reinforcement.

The *return on the investment* is computed by dividing the value of training by the cost of training. If you have followed the flow chart in Figure 2 to this point and if the return on the investment is positive and within the organization's guidelines, behavior modeling should be an appropriate method of training. If the return on the investment is not positive, then discontinue the project. (The entire procedure is illustrated in more detail at the conclusion of the following case example.)

AN EXAMPLE: THE COMMON CHEMICAL COMPANY

The Common Chemical Company (CCC), wanted to improve the selection-interview skills of its front-line supervisors. The supervisors interviewed job applicants sent to them by the personnel department for the position of process operator. Their system was apparently faulty, because many of the process operators selected were inappropriate for the job. Some were too highly qualified and left the company after a few months on the job. Others were underqualified and required a tremendous training investment before they became skillful or before it became evident that they would not be able to develop the needed skills. The hiring data showed that one-third of all newly hired process operators resigned or were involuntarily terminated within the first six months on the job.

A task force, led by CCC's Training Director, Gary Hafner, was formed to look into the problem further. The task force determined that the front-line supervisors lacked the skills needed to obtain relevant data about job-related behaviors in a selection interview. After the task force studied the situation in depth, Gary developed a selection-interview workshop using behavior modeling. Here's how Gary and the task force answered each of the seven questions on the decision flow chart.

1. Could the Person Do It If His or Her Life Depended on It?

The task force was not sure if the supervisors could interview effectively if their lives depended on it. For one thing the supervisors had never been told how they should be handling selection interviews. To find the answer to this question, the task force decided to test the supervisors' ability to interview. They randomly selected six competent supervisors and asked Gary to describe the interviewing process to these supervisors. The supervisors were then observed in three interviews to determine how well they were using the process. The supervisors did not perform effectively in any of the interviews. The supervisors *wanted* to perform well, because they had been told that was the process to use and they were being observed. However, the task force concluded that the supervisors could not do it even if their lives depended on it.

2. Is It a Skill Deficiency?

The task force then had to determine whether or not the training need was a matter of knowledge deficiency or skill deficiency. The sample of supervisors had been told what to do and had been provided with an outline of the interviewing process, yet they were not able to demonstrate the skills. Therefore, it was determined that the deficiency was primarily one of skill rather than of knowledge.

3. Can You Identify the Behaviors Needed To Overcome the Skill Deficiency?

On Gary's recommendation, the task force consulted a firm that specialized in selection systems. The consultants demonstrated that the use of specific skills could increase the effectiveness of the selection interview. The skill areas they identified were (1) how to open the conversation, (2) how to ask specific questions, (3) how to pin down applicant behavior through follow-up questions, (4) how to manage the interview to obtain more information when needed, (5) how to control time when interviewing verbose applicants, and (6) how to maintain the applicant's self-esteem. Specific behaviors could be identified in each of these categories for the supervisors to use in the interviews.

4. Can a Positive, Credible Model Be Demonstrated?

The consulting firm had already developed a modeling film in which a manufacturing supervisor interviewed an applicant for a machinist position. The consultants believed this modeling display would be perceived as positive and credible by the supervisors. To test this assumption, the task force selected six supervisors not included in the original sample to take part in a pilot. In the pilot session, Gary explained the interviewing process to them and told them they would see a film of a supervisor doing an interview. The supervisors were asked to take notes on how the supervisor in the film handled the situation because they would be expected to use these skills in their next interviews with applicants.

During the discussion after the film, Gary asked the supervisors three questions.

1. Do you think such an interview could really have taken place?
2. Was the supervisor effective in conducting the interview?
3. Do you feel you could learn the same skills?

Five answered yes to Question 1, six answered yes to Question 2, and four responded affirmatively to Question 3.

The task force felt the information from the first and second questions indicated that the supervisors saw the model supervisor as credible and perceived the film as a real situation.

The four-to-two split on Question 3 was a problem. None of the supervisors had ever been exposed to training through behavior modeling. The split alerted the task force that approximately one-third of the supervisors could have concerns about their ability to learn the skills and that these concerns would have to be dealt with in the classroom. The task force decided to move ahead with this modeling display. In the early classroom sessions, Gary would monitor what percentage of the supervisors felt they could learn the skills. If the percentage dropped below sixty, the task force would then re-examine the applicability of the modeling display.

5. Can Each Learner Practice the Skill?

In this case, the answer was an easy yes. The task force considered two possibilities. One was to use real job applicants. They would be asked to come in for a half-day and be interviewed by participants in that day's class. The other possibility was to use simulated interviews: Staff members, other supervisors, or new employees would assume the roles of applicants. Either case would provide the supervisors an opportunity for skill practice. The task force did not have to select the method at this point, but the members felt that either would work.

6. Will the New Skills Be Reinforced?

The task force examined four items:

1. *Self-Reinforcement.* In the initial discussions with supervisors, the task force determined that the supervisors were quite concerned by the high turnover of new employees. The supervisors believed that the new selection skills would improve their decisions about job applicants and that this would result in better qualified employees and lower turnover. The task force believed this payoff would be reinforcing to the supervisors.

2. *Peer Reinforcement.* The decision to train all supervisors in the organization would encourage all of them to use the same skills. Therefore, peer reinforcement should result from this systematic training, because all supervisors would acquire the same skills and would have a common framework for sharing experiences.

3. *Management Reinforcement.* In examining opportunities for managers to provide reinforcement, the task force determined that managers could act as reinforcers and coaches. However, because the managers were not conducting selection interviews with supervisors, it was determined that it was impractical for the managers to become visible, positive models.

4. *Organizational Reinforcement.* In examining the rewards and punishments within the organization, the task force determined that the present systems would reinforce the new skills. Because the supervisors were already interviewing applicants, the new technique would require no additional time. Supervisors were, however, receiving very little feedback on the quality of the data gathered from their interviews, and this problem would have to be solved.

Obstacles to Reinforcement. There seemed to be two obstacles: one in the area of management reinforcement and the other in the area of organizational reinforcement. The management-reinforcement concern was that managers were not skillful enough to coach subordinate supervisors on handling selection interviews. They also lacked skill in providing reinforcement through recognition and praise. Therefore, a management-reinforcement skills-building workshop was established in which managers would be provided with:

- An overview of the selection process.
- An examination of the skills that supervisors would have to use.
- Practice in utilizing those skills.
- Extensive practice in developing coaching skills.
- Extensive practice in developing reinforcement skills.

The obstacle in the area of organizational reinforcement was that the supervisors received no feedback about either the quantity or the quality of data they obtained from selection interviews. To overcome this, the task force decided to have employee-relations (ER) managers provide the supervisors with feedback about the information obtained. The data from each interview would be discussed by an ER manager and the supervisor. In this discussion, the ER manager could point out the valuable information and explain why it was needed. If the supervisor had not collected sufficient data, the ER manager would coach the supervisor on how to obtain the proper information. The ER managers would participate in a one-day reinforcement workshop in which they would learn how to reinforce and coach.

7. Is It Cost Beneficial?

The organization was losing fifty of 150 new employees per year. Twenty-three supervisors, five managers, and three ER managers needed to be trained. Gary calculated the return on the investment in correcting the deficiency in this situation. Table 1 shows the calculations he presented to the task force.

Based on the analysis required by the decision flow chart, the task force recommended the new selection-interview program for supervisors. Upper management accepted the recommendation, and the program was implemented. One year after the training for supervisors, managers, and ER managers was completed, the loss of new employees had been reduced from fifty to twenty-nine. By the end of the second year, the loss was reduced to twenty-three.

Table 1. Cost/Benefit Analysis

A. Value of Deficiency Correction
  1. Cost of hiring new operators:

a. Hiring costs per new hire	$ 108.00
b. Training cost for each new hire	$ 1,500.00
	$ 1,608.00

  2. Number of additional new hires projected
     to be retained each year[a]   x 25

  3. Total cost savings per year in hiring costs $40,200.00

  4. Termination costs

a. Per person	$425	
b. Times decrease in termination[a]	x 25 =	$10,625.00
		$50,825.00

B. Cost of Training

a. Cost of performance analysis and needs analysis	No Cost[b]
b. Cost of task analysis	$ 3,000.00
c. Purchase of modeling films and other educational software	$ 6,100.00
d. Training of two instructors, including travel and lodging	$ 2,800.00
e. Training-time costs	
23 supervisors for two days	$ 4,327.00
5 managers for two days	$ 1,202.00
3 ER managers for one day	$ 360.00
f. Classroom costs	$ 152.00
	$17,941.00

$$\frac{\text{Value of Deficiency Correction}}{\text{Cost of Training}} = \text{Return on Investment}$$

$$\frac{\$50,825}{\$17,941} = 283\% \text{ Return on Investment}$$

---

[a]Before training, loss was fifty new hires per year. After training, loss is projected to be one-half of that or twenty-five per year. Therefore, the number of additional new hires to be retained is projected to be twenty-five. The number of terminations will decrease by twenty-five.

[b]Performance and needs analyses were completed as part of a longer, earlier study.

Management felt that this 42 percent decrease in loss for the first
year and 54 percent decrease in loss for the second year was ample
return on the investment. The selection-interview program was,
therefore, implemented on an ongoing basis.

Behavior modeling is an appropriate learning strategy when
answers to Questions 1 through 7 on the decision flow chart are yes.
Judicious use of the flow chart will assist any organization in using
behavior modeling where it is justified.

REFERENCE

Mager, R.F., & Pipe, P. *Analyzing performance problems.* Belmont, CA: Fearon,
1970.

3

Defining Objectives:
What Is Effective Behavior?

If you can't describe it in behavioral terms, don't try to teach it. This is a fundamental concept of behavior modeling. *Instructional objectives,* which describe the intended outcomes of the learning experience in behavioral terms, are necessary. These objectives must meet two criteria:

1. They must be based on the needs of the learner.
2. They must describe behavior that will enable the learner to handle a specific on-the-job situation successfully.

How can you determine what behavior is effective for a given situation? Should you sit down with a pencil and paper and describe what you would do in that situation? Should you ask effective people what they would do in such a situation? Should you watch people who are handling such situations? Should you ask people how they like to be treated when involved in such a situation? Should you read a book on how to handle such situations? Should you try out different behaviors and discover which ones work best?

The answer is "all of the above." However, there is an appropriate time and place to use each of these techniques. The following section provides the process and some of the methods often used in determining behavioral objectives for a behavior-modeling program (see Figure 3).

HOW TO DETERMINE
BEHAVIORAL OBJECTIVES

1. Given: Identification of skill deficiency. The first step is a needs analysis to identify the existence of a skill deficiency.[5] Correcting this deficiency will alleviate a performance problem or enable the organiza-

---

[5]The assumption here is that a needs analysis has already identified a skill deficiency and the target learners. Although this chapter does not deal with needs-analysis techniques, some helpful references include Byham (1971), Kirkpatrick (1971), Mager and Pipe (1970), Morrison (1976), and Odiorne (1970).

tion to maximize an opportunity. Both the skill deficiency and the specific group of employees who must learn the new skill must be identified.

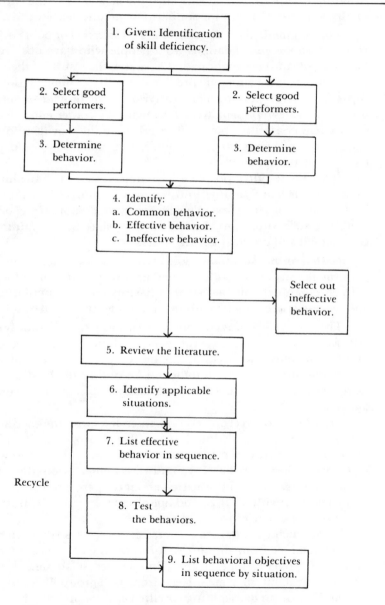

Figure 3. Process for Determining Behavioral Objectives

2. Select good performers and poor performers. Given an identified skill deficiency, the next activity in this process is to identify which employees are doing a good job and which are doing a poor job of handling the specific situation. Then the behaviors of the two groups can be analyzed to determine similarities and differences.

The best method for determining who are good or poor performers is to obtain recommendations from people who have observed their handling of similar situations and have seen the results of their efforts. For example, managers could provide you with recommendations about supervisors who report to them; supervisors could provide recommendations about sales representatives, sales managers, order-entry clerks, and other client-contact people. Staff members could provide information about line managers, and, of course, line managers could provide recommendations about staff.

Ask your resource people to recommend several individuals who can effectively handle a situation of concern to you. At the same time ask for the names of several people who generally do *not* do a good job in handling such situations. Your goal is to start with a minimum of twelve good and twelve poor performers.

3. Determine behavior. Collect information on how the good performers and poor performers handle the situation. This information will be compiled into a list of behaviors so that similarities and differences between the two groups can be identified and examined.

There are several ways to collect this information. Certainly the best way is to observe directly the good and poor performers. Direct observation offers an accurate picture of what actually takes place during the interaction. An audiotape recording of the discussion is extremely useful, because it allows analysis of the interaction at a later date.

In addition to direct observation, interviews with the good and poor performers are essential. Interviews with the people with whom the good and poor performers interact and interviews with their immediate superiors are also essential. If you use direct observation, the interview can provide *additional* information about the perceptions and feelings of the people involved. If you do not observe directly, the interview is your *primary* source of information.

I recommend a *patterned interview* in all cases, so that comparable data are obtained from all sources. Although the patterned interview is structured differently for each group interviewed, it is designed to obtain information about the same subjects from each group. In all interviews the emphasis is on determining specific behavior and the rationale for using that behavior. The interview does not seek information about management philosophies, management styles, or general concepts of management. See Figure 4 for an example of a patterned interview.

The patterned interview with the good and poor performers zeros in on what they actually do during the interaction and why. It also obtains information on what they would like to have done differently if they had been able to do so.

The patterned interview with the other people in the interaction focuses on the effectiveness of the discussion from their points of view. It also focuses on the behaviors employed by both parties during the interaction and seeks information about what they wish had happened differently during the discussion.

The interview with the managers of the good and poor performers concentrates on those areas in which the managers feel they do especially well and those areas in which they need improvement and on the reasons for the good and poor performances.

I am going to mention several situations that you, a supervisor, may face on the job. I would like you to tell me how you handle each of these situations:

(1) One of your employees, who is normally a good performer, has been making more than the standard number of errors during the last two weeks.

A. When would you first approach the employee?

B. Think of an actual situation in which you discussed poor quality of work with an employee. Tell me what happened in that discussion—both what you said and what the employee said.

C. What would you do differently if you could have that discussion again?

D. What was the employee's reaction to the discussion?

E. Did the employee's performance change? How?

(2) After a first discussion with the employee, the number of errors remain the same. Describe how you would handle the second discussion.

A. When would you again approach the employee?

B. Think of an actual situation of this type that you have handled. Tell me what happened in that discussion—both what you said and what the employee said.

C. What would you do differently if you could have that discussion again?

D. What was the employee's reaction to the discussion?

E. Did the employee's performance change? How?

Figure 4. Sample Patterned Interview

---

4. Identify common, effective, and ineffective behaviors. To make comparisons, you need a list of the behaviors used by both the good and poor performers (see Table 1). This list should also show how often each behavior was used. For example, if nine of the twelve good performers used a particular behavior, the list should indicate that it was used 75 percent of the time.

In addition to data about the frequency of the behaviors, a qualitative description of the behaviors is needed. For example, it is normal to find that both good and poor performers use the same behaviors in the same type of interaction. However, there usually is a significant difference in the quality of those behaviors. Descriptors can help to identify the quality of the behavior (see Table 2 for examples).

Table 2. Example of Frequency and Qualitative Description of Behaviors

General Behavior
Discussion of Possible Solutions

Specific Behaviors	**Frequency of Specific Behaviors**	
	Good Performers	Poor Performers
Good Performer		
1. Asked employee for solutions.	80%	25%
2. Introduced additional solutions.	65%	15%
3. Encouraged two-way discussion.	85%	50%
4. Encouraged building on each other's ideas, thus improving solutions.	60%	10%
5. Encouraged discussion with nonverbal signals.	75%	40%
Poor Performer		
1. Did not ask employee for solutions.	20%	75%
2. Gave solutions without asking for solutions.	20%	75%
3. Used intimidating tone of voice.	15%	50%
4. Used aggressive nonverbals.	20%	50%

Once the frequency and the quality have been determined, the behaviors should be sorted into three categories: common, effective, and ineffective.

Common Behaviors. These are the behaviors common to both the good and poor performers, both in quality and frequency. That is, both good and poor performers demonstrate these behaviors. This is vital information to the development of the training software. It means that all the participants in the classroom (both good and poor performers) can be expected to have these skills before training. Therefore, they will not have a training need for these specific skills. Of course, there may be a need for them to learn how to coordinate these skills with other skills that they will be learning in the training program.

Effective Behaviors. Effective behaviors are those utilized by the majority of the good performers. One criterion for selecting effective behavior is the judgment of the "recipient" in the interaction that this type of behavior moved the discussion forward in a positive manner. The managers of the performers should also be asked what behaviors moved the discussion forward.

It is much more difficult to determine from the good and poor performers themselves what behaviors they used to move the discussion forward. Certainly the poor performers are not utilizing very many effective behaviors. However, even good performers find it difficult to distinguish which of their behaviors are really effective and which are not. The best sources for determining effective and ineffective behavior are the managers of the target audience and the people with whom the target audience interacts.

Some effective behaviors will also be found in the poor-performer group. The key to identifying these effective behaviors is whether or not they moved the discussion along in a positive manner.

Ineffective Behaviors. Ineffective behaviors are usually the easiest to spot. They are behaviors that caused the discussion to break down or slow down. The ineffective behaviors usually have a negative effect on the recipient. They cause the discussion to get off track or to regress so there is no movement toward resolution. Some ineffective behaviors will also be found in the good-performer group.

The next step is to remove the ineffective behaviors from the list. They will not be a part of the final behavioral objectives. However, they should be kept with the needs-analysis data so that the modeling display can be checked against them to make sure that it does not portray any ineffective behaviors.

The common behaviors and effective behaviors should be arranged in a list for Step 7, in which the effective behaviors will be arranged in sequence.

5. *Review the literature.* The purpose of the literature review is to identify behaviors for a given situation that are advocated by experts in the field. For example, if you are concerned with setting and reviewing performance goals, examine the literature on management by objectives, goal setting, goal negotiation, and goals review and renegotiation. Look for information about interactions between managers and their subordinates as they set and review performance goals. In reviewing the literature, you have the responsibility to extract the effective behaviors, as advocated by the experts, for handling the specific situations identified in your front-end analysis. In doing this, you would normally use the behaviors that have the greatest research support and that refer to a population most closely resembling your target audience.

The end result of a literature review is a list of effective behaviors and a list of ineffective behaviors. These lists are different from the lists derived from observation and interviews.

6. Identify applicable situations. The observations, interviews, and literature review will uncover a variety of conditions under which the skills have been used. A list should be made of all the conditions, i.e., the situations in which the skills have been applied. For example, if the skill being considered were "setting performance goals," the types of situations uncovered could be the following:

- Manager with supervisor.
- Supervisor with employee.
- Supervisor with work team.
- Senior manager with middle manager.
- All goals negotiable.
- Goals not negotiable.
- Some goals negotiable and some not negotiable.
- Maximum control over resources.
- Minimum control over resources.

Some of these situations will *not* apply to the target audience and, therefore, will be eliminated. The remaining situations will be used in the next three steps.

7. List effective behaviors in sequence. The task now is to determine which behaviors would be effective for handling each one of the applicable situations and to arrange them in sequence. For each situation, first examine the behaviors classified as effective. Then examine the behaviors common to both effective and ineffective performers. Next list the common and the effective behaviors in sequence. In most cases, a preliminary sequence will already be established from the information obtained through observations, interviews, and literature reviews. An observer watches the behavior in sequence, and people can be asked to list an effective-behavior sequence during the interview. Most likely the literature also will offer examples of sequences of behavior.

Because too many behaviors will probably emerge, the next step is to establish which behaviors are not essential, that is, which could be eliminated without causing a significant reduction in one's effectiveness in handling the situation. The remaining behaviors should then be listed succinctly. This list forms the *critical steps* for the skill to be learned. Critical steps are purposely worded simply and succinctly so that they can be easily understood and used as a check list, both in the classroom and on the job. An example of critical steps is shown in Figure 5.

---

1. Describe the problem in a friendly manner.
2. Ask for the employee's help in solving the problem.
3. Discuss causes of the problem.
4. Identify and write down possible solutions.
5. Decide on specific actions to be taken by each of you.
6. Agree on a specific follow-up date.

Figure 5. Critical Steps for Improving Employee Performance

Critical steps should be developed for each situation that has been identified, so that a list of succinct behaviors (expressed as critical steps) is applicable for each situation.

From time to time, you may feel that the observations, interviews, and literature review have not provided you with enough examples of effective behavior to structure an entire sequence for a particular situation. For example, you may be looking for situations in which supervisors have successfully overcome resentment by members of their work groups. You might have found only one or two instances of effective performance from your observations and interviews. In addition, your review of the literature might not have yielded examples that are appropriate for your organization. In such cases, conduct more observations and interviews until you can determine what behaviors are effective for that situation. Otherwise, you will violate one of the precepts of the behavior-modeling approach: If you can't describe it in behavioral terms, don't try to teach it.

If your literature review reveals that some authors advocate behaviors that other authors reject, this dilemma rests entirely on your shoulders. You must compare what is taking place in the real world with what the authors advocate. Then you must decide which of the routes suggested by the authors is closest to the behavior that enables the learner to handle the situation effectively in real life. Although this decision is your responsibility, it is not irrevocable. In fact, Step 8 tests the behaviors for effectiveness.

8. Test the behaviors. Once the critical steps have been determined, the behaviors must be tested. The best way to do this is through a behavioral demonstration.

If, for instance, you were developing skills in introducing change and overcoming resistance to change, you would set up several behavioral demonstrations, in which people representative of the target audience could test the critical steps. If, for example, the target audience were supervisors, you would select at least six competent supervisors and ask them to participate in the behavioral demonstration. To begin the demonstration, you would tell each supervisor that the purpose of the demonstration was to test the critical steps for introducing change and handling resistance to change. You would describe the variety of situations being tested. The critical steps for introducing change, for example, could be applicable in the following situations:

- A change that involves only one person.
- A change that involves the entire work team.
- A change that allows no opportunities to modify the plan.
- A change that allows the work team to help plan the implementation.
- A change that allows the work team to determine that change, provided the intended outcomes are met.

After explaining the different situations, instruct a supervisor to select a situation similar to one he or she actually faces on the job. The intent is to have a competent supervisor use the critical steps to handle an actual on-the-job situation. Select someone to take the role of the subordinate. This "subordinate" may be a peer supervisor or program-development staff member who understands the situation and can respond as a typical subordinate.

During the behavioral demonstration, the "supervisor" handles the situation with the "subordinate" by following the critical steps, and the discussion is audiotaped. At least six behavioral demonstrations with competent supervisors are conducted. The demonstrations deal with the same set of conditions, but each supervisor selects an on-the-job situation with which he or she is familiar. The same critical steps are used each time.

This process takes place for each of the applicable situations. If there were four applicable situations, behavioral demonstrations by at least six competent supervisors for each of the four situations would be conducted.

After the demonstrations, analyze the audiotapes to determine the effectiveness of each critical step. An *error analysis* can be used to determine which critical steps presented problems for the supervisor or at what points the discussion seemed to be ineffective. This analysis highlights errors in the critical steps and thus identifies those that must be modified. It also identifies those that provided an effective discussion.

The error analysis provides data not only for modifying the critical steps, but also for combining or eliminating applicable situations. Applicable situations that initially appear unique can sometimes be handled with the same set of critical steps after the first series of behavioral demonstrations. Therefore, any applicable situations that can be handled with the same set of critical steps are combined into a single situation. Note that only the *critical steps* are the same; the *situations* that the participants need practice in handling are different.

Sometimes participants in the behavioral demonstration will indicate that one of the applicable situations is not a problem or does not occur in real life. If this happens and if these individuals are representative of the target audience, conduct a follow-up needs analysis. If that additional analysis reveals that the situation does not occur, it can be eliminated.

In addition to combining and eliminating situations, the behaviors themselves should also be re-examined. Recycle them through Step 7 for modifications if they appear to be in error. Information on how to modify them can be obtained from participants in the demonstrations, from more observations and interviews, or from a more in-depth review of the literature. After you have revised the critical steps, test them again by using another round of demonstrations (Step 8). Anayze these again and, depending on the results, either move to Step 9 or modify the behaviors again.

One purpose of testing behaviors (Step 8) is to simplify the process as much as possible. For best results, the behaviors should consist of no more than eight critical steps. Step 8 also reduces the number of applicable situations by combining situations with identical critical steps and by eliminating the ones that do not occur frequently. By the time Step 9 is reached, the critical steps should be succinct and easily understood.

9. List behavioral objectives in sequence by situation. As mentioned at the beginning of this chapter, behavioral objectives must be based on the needs of the learner and must describe behavior that will enable the learner to handle a specific on-the-job situation successfully. The first eight steps have produced these objectives, and now they should be listed in sequence by situation.

The following example follows the process to completion and gives illustrations of behavioral objectives.

AN EXAMPLE: THE GWS CORPORATION

The GWS Corporation is a medium-sized manufacturer of electronic components. It operates two plants in the United States, one in the Southeast and another on the West Coast. The plants have a combined work force of approximately one thousand employees, including seventy-five first-line supervisors, twenty-five second-level managers, and fifteen middle- and upper-level managers.

1. Given: Identification of skill deficiency. An employee survey conducted in both plants revealed that employees were satisfied with working conditions, employee benefits, and wages. They were unhappy with supervision. Their major complaint was that the supervisors were not sufficiently responsive to employee concerns and complaints.

In checking into this complaint, the training director, Lynn Hauck, discovered the following factors:

- When employees brought complaints to supervisors, they felt the supervisors showed only superficial interest.
- Although supervisors were not comfortable with the way they were handling complaints, they did not know of a better method.
- Second- and third-level managers, to whom complaints were being referred, often felt the complaints should have been handled by first-line supervisors.
- Complaints were being brought to the personnel department by employees, and personnel managers felt that these complaints should have been handled by supervisors.

Further analysis indicated:

- Supervisors could not handle the complaints effectively, even if their lives depended on it.
- The major reason for their failure to handle the complaints was skill deficiency.

Because a skill deficiency existed, Lynn Hauck proceeded to use the process outlined in this chapter for determining behavioral objectives.

2. Select good and poor performers. Lynn started her behavioral-data collection by first selecting good and poor performers in the area of handling employee complaints. She asked the managers, the personnel managers, and key employees to identify twelve supervisors thought to be effective in handling employee complaints and twelve thought to be ineffective.

3. Determine behaviors. Lynn and her staff conducted patterned interviews to collect data about supervisors' behaviors. These interviews with first-line supervisors, managers, and employees focused on the type of complaint received and how the supervisor handled each type.

It was not possible to observe the supervisors directly as they handled employee complaints. Because the complaints were employee initiated, they occurred sporadically without being anticipated. Some discussions were confidential. Because there was no way to determine the need for confidentiality at the onset of the complaint, all had to be treated as though they were confidential.

Lynn felt another way of obtaining real data would be to simulate complaints and audiotape them. The idea was to have the good and poor performers agree to being audiotaped while a staff member directed a simulated complaint to them. Lynn tried four of these simulations, with minimal success. Everyone involved, including the supervisors, felt that the simulations lacked credibility and seemed artificial. Lynn and her staff agreed that further simulations would not provide usable data. Therefore, the only usable data were from the patterned interviews.

4. Identify common, effective, and ineffective behaviors. When the interviews were completed, Lynn and her staff had information from twenty supervisors (eleven good performers and nine poor performers), eight second-level supervisors, four third-level supervisors, and twenty subordinates (one for each first-line supervisor).

The behaviors were then separated into three categories: behaviors common to both good and poor performers, effective behaviors, and ineffective behaviors. Table 3 shows some of the behaviors under each category.

The common behaviors and the effective behaviors were later incorporated into the critical steps. The ineffective behaviors were later used as guidelines for ruling out certain behaviors in the modeling display.

5. Review the literature. Lynn discovered that many of the common behaviors were identified in the literature as effective behaviors. In addition to the specific behaviors determined by the patterned interview, her review of the literature suggested that two other general behaviors make complaint handling more effective:

- Maintaining the self-esteem of the person lodging the complaint. For example, the supervisor can express

Table 3. GWS Corporation's Categories of Behaviors

General Behavior
 Handling Complaints

Frequency of Specific Behaviors
 GoodPoor

Specific Behaviors	Performers	Performers
Common		
1. Listens to complaints.	100%	80%
2. Obtains all details of complaints.	100%	80%
Effective		
1. Listens intently.	90%	20%
2. Shows understanding of employee's point of view.	65%	-0-
3. Discusses possible solutions.	90%	5%
4. Indicates next step.	100%	35%
Ineffective		
1. Becomes defensive	-0-	60%
2. Tries to justify the situation.	25%	95%
3. Becomes argumentative.	-0-	55%
4. Indicates nothing can be done.	10%	85%

appreciation to the subordinate for bringing the problem to his or her attention.

● Indicating that the complainant's feelings at that time are understood. This is especially important because a subordinate may feel guilty about bringing a complaint to a supervisor or may feel hostile toward that supervisor.

6. Identify applicable situations. Of the various situations mentioned in the patterned interviews, four occurred most frequently:

1. The routine complaint, about a situation directly affecting the employee or fellow employees.
2. The complaint in which an employee becomes emotional because of a situation affecting him or her.
3. A complaint of alleged discrimination.
4. A complaint lodged by a group of employees.

Also, several managers and supervisors felt that supervisors would be required to use different skills, depending on whether the complaint was lodged by a female or male.

7. List effective behaviors in sequence. Lynn and her staff listed effective behaviors for each of the four situations they had identified in Step 6. They decided to test the recommended behaviors with both male and female employees to determine whether or not supervisors needed to employ different behaviors with males and females. For example, the effective behaviors for handling a routine complaint were sequentially listed as:

1. Listen intently.
2. Respond with empathy.
3. Obtain all the details of the complaint.
4. Show that the situation is understood.
5. Openly present your position.
6. Mutually agree on follow-up action.
7. Set a specific follow-up date.
8. Thank the complainant for bringing the problem to your attention.

8. Test the behaviors. To test the behaviors, six supervisors considered effective in handling employee complaints were selected from each plant. Most had participated in the patterned interview. None had participated in the earlier simulations.

Two staff trainers (a male and a female) were assigned to each supervisor. For the first three situations, one trainer described the behaviors in detail. The behaviors were also listed on a chart. Both trainers demonstrated how a supervisor would handle each type of complaint and then asked the supervisor to handle a complaint from each trainer while the other trainer observed. This helped determine whether different behaviors were required for complainants of different genders.

For the fourth situation, a complaint by a group of employees, one trainer demonstrated handling a complaint from four employees. The supervisor was then asked to handle a complaint from the same four employees. In each case, two of the employees were male and two were female.

As a result of these behavioral demonstrations, Lynn's staff modified the critical steps for all four situations. The demonstrations also indicated there was no need to employ different behaviors for complainants of different genders. The modifications in the critical steps for a routine complaint were as follows:

- Behavior 3 was changed to read: "Obtain all the details of the complaint and make notes." This was necessary because the employees perceived supervisors as more interested when they made notes of the complaint.
- Behavior 6 was changed to read: "Decide on specific follow-up action." This was necessary because many times the supervisor and employee could not attain mutual agreement on the issue. Trying to arrive at a mutual agreement became a waste of time and was frustrating for both. Under these circumstances, it was the responsibility of the supervisor to decide on the specific action.

The modified behaviors were tested in another round of behavioral demonstrations and worked satisfactorily in each case.

9. List behavioral objectives in sequence by situation. Lynn and her staff also determined that the behaviors for handling a routine complaint by one employee (not an emotional situation or a discrimination complaint) were the same ones required for handling a group complaint. The behaviors needed to handle an emotional situation and a discrimination complaint, however, were significantly different; each required a separate set of behavioral objectives.

The following behavioral objectives were determined to be effective for handling routine complaints, whether lodged by an individual or a group. These behavioral objectives were presented in simple, succinct language so they could be easily understood and remembered by supervisors:

1. Listen intently and respond with empathy to the employee.
2. Obtain all the details of the complaint and make notes.
3. Respond by showing that you understand the situation.
4. Openly present your position.
5. Decide on specific action and a follow-up date.
6. Thank the employee for bringing the complaint to your attention.

Determining the effective behavior for a given situation is a time-consuming process that requires painstaking attention to detail. The magnitude and the complexity of the process have frustrated many a training professional. However, the precise determination of the effective behavior is crucial. A fundamental concept of behavior modeling is

"If you can't describe it in behavioral terms, don't try to teach it." Effective behavior must be completely and accurately specified if a behavior-modeling program is to succeed.

Certainly there are shortcuts to the process outlined in this chapter. Nevertheless, each shortcut increases the probability of error. Such errors will eventually show up in the classroom or as supervisors and managers attempt to use the skills on the job.

REFERENCES

Byham, W.C. The assessment center as an aid in management development. *Training and Development Journal*, 1971, *25*(12), 10-21.

Kirkpatrick, D. *Practical guide for supervisory training and development*. Reading, MA: Addison-Wesley, 1971.

Mager, R.F., & Pipe, P. *Analyzing performance problems*. Belmont, CA: Fearon, 1970.

Morrison, J.H. Determining training needs. In R.L. Craig (Ed.), *Training and development handbook* (2nd ed.). New York: McGraw-Hill, 1976.

Odiorne, G.S. *Training by objectives*. New York: Macmillan, 1970.

4

Creating a Modeling Display: The Grapple Tapes

George Grapple had been a training specialist for a utility company before accepting the position of management-development manager of the Tom-Lee Corporation.

One of his first challenges at Tom-Lee was to develop a training program for front-line supervisors. George conducted a needs analysis, which showed that supervisors could be effective if they were more skillful in nine specific areas of supervisor-employee interactions. In his former position, George had been an instructor in the behavior-modeling program for supervisors, and he knew what behavior modeling could accomplish.

George decided to develop a behavior-modeling program for Tom-Lee. After all, he was experienced in behavior modeling. He knew firsthand which supervisory skills and what software were needed. He still had his old instructor's manual, so he knew he could readily borrow material from the utility company's program and adapt it to the Tom-Lee situation.

George decided to start with the development of modeling displays—videotapes. By using the in-house videotape capability and asking Tom-Lee supervisors to be the models, George could produce the videotapes at very little cost.

The first videotape George decided to develop was "Discussing Quality of Work with an Employee." He examined the critical steps in the utility company's program and decided that they would be appropriate with only minor editing.

George remembered the utility company's tape vividly; it was a good modeling display. But now that he was in a manufacturing organization, he knew he would have to use a different setting. He had observed several quality-of-work problems during his needs analysis, and he selected a common one: poor-quality in-house printing. He chose a situation in which a supervisor had to deal with a press operator who did not meet the company's quality standards.

George decided that the easiest way to produce the modeling display was to use the print-shop supervisor as the model. George thought he needed only to outline the critical steps to the print-shop supervisor and ask him to follow them in handling the problem. He decided also to use one of the print-shop employees so that the modeling display would be more realistic. The print-shop supervisor and one of the press operators agreed to do the tape. To add more realism to the modeling display, George decided to tape at the press in the print shop.

Tuesday evening at seven o'clock, George, the video-production crew, the print-shop supervisor, and the press operator began producing the first modeling display. By nine o'clock George realized that the print-shop supervisor was not going to follow the critical steps, despite the many times George had coached him. The supervisor already had established a way of dealing with poor-quality printing, and he insisted on using this method. At 9:45, George completed the videotaping. He thanked the print-shop supervisor, the press operator, and the videotape crew. As the production crew left, they gave George the tape, which he decided to throw away.

The next morning, George realized that all was not lost. Even though the print-shop supervisor did not follow the critical steps, George at least had the situation, issues, and problems to be addressed in the next videotape. All he really needed was another supervisor to handle these issues and problems and follow the critical steps.

George asked two other managers to help him with the videotape. One was an effective manager, who agreed to use the critical steps and be the model supervisor. The other, who had come up through the ranks, agreed to be the subordinate. George chose the company's film studio as the taping site and scheduled an early-morning production. Since the lighting in the studio was designed for videotaping, the quality of this tape should be greatly improved.

The taping started promptly at 8:15 a.m., with George directing the model supervisor and subordinate to handle the entire discussion without interruption. George felt the discussion could have gone better at several points if the participants had handled it differently. Rather than interrupt the taping, however, he waited and coached them on everything he wanted done differently.

The second take also proceeded without interruption, but George again felt a few things needed to be changed, so he coached the models a bit more and asked them to try again. Two minutes into the third videotaping, the supervisor asked to start again. About three minutes into the fourth videotaping, George realized this was the worst take so far. From there on things steadily declined. Finally, at 11:15 a.m.,

George decided they had done enough. He was not sure he had any takes that were as good as he wanted, so he thanked the two managers for their help and told them he wanted to view the tapes before deciding which one to use.

The model supervisor admitted he had been very nervous from the third take on. He felt the first couple of takes had gone well because he conducted the discussion his way. Because of George's coaching and the presence of the camera, the supervisor became tense and was unable to perform well. George agreed that being on camera for the first time could be difficult but expressed optimism that the session had been productive.

After viewing the tapes, George realized he still did not have a modeling display he could use. He thought he could solve the problem by asking two people in the training department to do the videotape. The trainers ought to feel comfortable doing it, because they were used to being on camera. George planned to coach them in advance about the details of the print-shop problem. Because trainers were accustomed to being coached, George believed he could tape a realistic modeling display without experiencing the problems he had with the other employees. The third taping session was scheduled for the next Friday afternoon. George scheduled a briefing for Wednesday to give both the "supervisor" and the "employee" an opportunity to study their parts and to rehearse. The rehearsals were encouraging, and George was optimistic about the next videotape.

On Friday, the taping started as planned at 1:25 p.m. After the first take, George felt he now had something that was almost good enough. He and the trainers talked about the minor flaws, agreed on some changes, and then went into a second take. The second take was even better than the first. This time George had a videotape he could use. He and the trainers discussed the second take and decided to try for a third that would contain two or three modifications. At 3:00 p.m., they shot the third take, which proved to be the best. He thanked the trainers and the production crew. He knew he had something he could use in the classroom.

George continued and produced eight more videotapes. The procedure was the same for each: He obtained the issues and problems from a person who actually worked in the job and then used training-department employees to perform for the display.

Three months later, George was ready to conduct his first behavior-modeling workshop, and he was quite proud of his accomplishment. However, when the first three groups of supervisors went through the first module, "Discussing Quality of Work with an Employee," he began to hear critical comments about the modeling displays:

- "The guys in the tapes don't talk like supervisors."
- "Boy, Claude must really be acting, because he sure doesn't handle himself that way in real life."
- "In Critical Step 3, Claude didn't give the employee an opportunity to talk, even though it said to discuss the subject in detail."
- "It sure looks like that tape was done in a studio. I wonder why they didn't have the discussion at the press."

George was disappointed. He thought the tapes were quite good. He thought they were as good as the ones in the utility company's program. He asked himself:

- How can I make a credible modeling display?
- How can I locate the talent to demonstrate the correct dose of positive behavior?
- How can I evaluate a modeling display to determine if it will be perceived as credible?

This chapter attempts to answer those questions. If George still wants to produce his own modeling displays, this chapter may be of help.

CREATING CREDIBLE MODELS

The purpose of the modeling display is to demonstrate to the learner how a skillful person handles a situation effectively. Three specific questions (as discussed in Chapters 1 and 2) should be kept in mind when producing a modeling display. Each must be answered in the affirmative *by the target audience:*

1. Could the situation I just viewed have happened in real life?
2. Did the model handle the situation effectively?
3. Could I learn to do the same thing?

A yes to each question means the modeling display is credible. The process for meeting those criteria requires developing the critical steps (as outlined in Chapter 3) into a modeling display. The process is outlined in Figure 6 and detailed in the following sections.

1. Script Outline

The first step in producing a modeling display is preparing the script outline, which should touch on all the pertinent information about the modeling display—including descriptions of the setting, the characters, and the behaviors to be demonstrated under each critical step. The script

---

Given: Critical Steps

1. Script Outline
2. Script Preparation
3. Talent Selection/Management
4. Prototype Modeling Display
5. Field Test
6. Final Modeling Display

Figure 6. Steps in Creating a Modeling Display

---

outline generally has the following components. (Ways to incorporate these components into the outline are included.):

Context. Define the position of the modeling display in the sequence of the learning experience. Describe in detail the learning activities that occur just before and after viewing the modeling display, and position the skill module within the context of the entire program. Provide an overview of the entire program, describing the target audience, the modules within the program, and the program objectives.

Critical Steps. Define the critical steps to be presented in the modeling display.

Generic Skills. If *generic skills* are part of the overall program, describe where and how they fit into this modeling display.

Setting. Describe the setting, including the physical location of the action, the job title of each person, and where each person fits into the organization.

Issues. Describe the main theme, along with the major issues or problems that will be addressed in the modeling display.

The Model. Describe the characteristics of the model, including age, race, gender, technical background, position, and responsibilities.

Other People. Describe the characteristics of the other people in the display, including age, race, gender, technical background, position, and responsibility.

Behavior by Critical Step. This is the most crucial and difficult part of the script outline. Each behavior of each person in the modeling display must be outlined for each critical step. This outline is needed to plan completely the scenario before any scripting takes place and to make sure the behaviors called for by the critical steps are shown in the modeling display. Express the behaviors as actions, reactions, and emotions. The behaviors also outline the content (issues and problems) to be dealt with under each critical step. See Figure 7 for an example of behaviors by critical step.

| | BEHAVIOR | |
CRITICAL STEP	SUPERVISOR	EMPLOYEE
1. Listen intently and respond with empathy to the complainant.	1.2 Says that's O.K. (calm).	1.1 Asks to talk (slightly nervous).
	1.4 Asks open-ended questions (calm).	(sits).
	1.6 Asks for example (calm).	1.5 Complains vaguely about supervisors (slight anger).
	1.8 Acknowledges employee's anger (shows empathy).	1.7 Complains that another employee, Tom, leaves common work area a mess (shows anger).
2. Obtain all the details of the complaint and make notes.	2.1 Asks for details: when, where (takes notes).	
	2.3 Asks if other day-shift employees have similar problems (questions).	2.2 Says Tom works night shift; every morning a mess (sarcastic).
	2.5 (Calm) Asks how long it has happened (takes notes).	2.4 Replies no, just his work area (anger).
	2.7 Summarizes data provided by employee (shows empathy).	2.6 Says one month (ventilates); describes type of mess: "need road map."

Figure 7. Behavior by Critical Step: Handling Employee Complaints

2. Script Preparation

The script is like an architect's building plan. Just as poor architectural drawings lead to unsound buildings, so a poor script generates an ineffective modeling display.

There seems to be no uniform approach to script writing. Some people write the original script, strictly following the script outline. Others recruit people from work environments similar to those described in the scripts, audiotape several behavioral demonstrations, and base their scripts on these tapes.

Many times two script writers work together; one provides the content and describes the process, and the other generates the dialog.

Regardless of the approach, the objective is to develop a script that:

- Is understandable to the target audience.
- Uses the same language as does the target audience.
- Has a high degree of realism.
- Vividly displays the desired behavior.

3. Talent Selection/Management

When building a home, a carpenter knows that the final structure can be no better than the raw materials. Similarly, no videotape is better than the talent it uses.

Is it better to hire professional actors or to use skillful employees of the organization that will use the tape? Many directors of modeling displays claim they obtain best results from professional talent. Other directors say in-house people who are familiar with the situation are better. It is a debate that will continue for years. Nevertheless, some guidelines on the process are offered in this chapter, and the advantages and disadvantages of using professional and nonprofessional talent will be discussed. Whether the talent is professional or nonprofessional, the process for selecting and managing the talent is the same.

Proper selection is crucial. Although professionals generally have experience in commercials, comedies, and dramas, acting in a modeling display requires behaviors that are unique. Unless they have acted in previous modeling displays, your professional talent will need to be coached in these unfamiliar behaviors. The same holds true for nonprofessionals. The nonprofessional—an in-house manager, for instance—will be asked to display behaviors that are often very different from those used on the real job. Therefore, in selecting talent, look for a person who:

- Will take direction.
- Will memorize lines.
- Can understand the situation, issues, and problems.
- Will work hard to produce the final product as the director wants it.
- Has good oral-communication skills, i.e., voice quality, enunciation, and expression.
- Demonstrates the kind of nonverbal behavior needed in the film.

If you can find the right talent, you have a good chance of producing an effective modeling display. Having talent with previous experience is always helpful. A person who has experience in front of a camera will be less inhibited and less likely to stutter or forget lines.

After the actors are selected, they must be managed to produce the best possible modeling display. This can be accomplished by:

- Thoroughly briefing them on performance expectations.
- Coaching them in the desired behaviors.
- Evaluating each take.
- Providing them with feedback.
- Insisting on retakes until a satisfactory product is achieved.

4. Prototype Modeling Display

The objective of producing a prototype is to produce a relatively inexpensive modeling display for field testing *(formative evaluation)*. The main concern for the prototype is how well and how accurately the talent portray the behaviors. There is less concern with the technical quality of the videotape or film. Most people use videotape for prototype modeling displays. It is relatively inexpensive, because it requires a small production crew, yet its quality is satisfactory for field tests. Videotape can also be edited with reasonable accuracy.

Detailed planning with both the production crew and the talent is required before the camera can roll. The talent may need coaching and directing, and a technical director can be appointed to be responsible for the production crew.

Several weeks before shooting the scenes, review the script outline with the technical director and decide on all the details. Later, after the script is finalized, review the script to plan each scene, camera angles, and the final schedule.

Brief the talent so they thoroughly understand the situation, including the critical steps, the tasks, the generic skills, the content, the problem to be resolved, and the setting of the vignette. Review the script in detail. The professional actors may think that discussions between a manager and a subordinate are characterized by confrontation rather than by support and mutual problem solving. Before the actors rehearse the script, they must understand the feelings of each person in the script and the climate in the situation.

The actual filming or taping is one of the highlights of behavior-modeling program development. So much time and planning go into the process up to this point that a real feeling of accomplishment is present when the camera finally begins to roll.

During the shooting, organization is crucial. Salaries of the production crew and fees for talent and equipment can become expensive. Good organization will make both the talent and the production crew more efficient.

Film or video directing requires a lot of skill and experience. If you have never directed a film, enlist the aid of someone who is experienced.

5. Field Test

This step is very exciting. By this time, it has taken several weeks or months of hard work to develop the prototype modeling display; now it is time to find out whether or not it is effective. The objectives of the field test are the following:

- To determine whether the critical steps can be put into practice by the learners.
- To determine whether the behavior of the model is perceived as credible and effective by the learners.
- To determine whether the setting of the modeling display is understandable and realistic to the learners.

The field test must be structured to provide specific recommendations about the behavior of the models, the effectiveness of the critical steps, and the appropriateness of the setting and situation. Some standardized instrument must be used, so that feedback from all field-test groups will be complete and deal with the same issues. In addition, the field-test instrument must be designed to solicit both positive and negative feedback and encourage recommendations for changes.

There are generally three different sources of data during the field test: the target audience, experienced instructors, and higher management.

Target Audience. In field testing with the target audience, the viewers should be unaware, until after their participation, that the material is being field tested. The participants must perceive the field test as a regularly scheduled workshop. They should not be aware that they are evaluating a new program. Therefore, in setting up the field test, select participants who are representative of the target audience and schedule them for what appears to be a complete workshop. That workshop could consist of several prototype modeling displays and some completed modules. Even though the primary purpose is to test only the modeling display, the field test will be ineffective unless the participants hear the introduction, view the prototype modeling display, participate in skill practice, receive feedback, and hear the instructor's closing comments.

The field-test workshop must be conducted by a skillful instructor with a thorough knowledge of both the process and the content. During the workshop, an observer should be present to take notes on the learning that takes place and the participants' reactions. The observer's job is to record data (behavior and reactions) rather than to draw conclusions, and he or she should be provided with an evaluation instrument.

Not only does the observer record information about the prototype model, but also about the other educational software, such as the skill-practice exercises and background reading, used in the field test.

Instructors. Many times an organization has instructors who have already conducted modeling programs and who are familiar with the modeling process, the generic skills, and even the program objectives. This field test allows a skillful instructor to conduct complete modules and other instructors to participate as though they were managers. Showing only the prototype modeling display is ineffective. Again, a reliable observer should record data on the evaluation sheets.

Higher Management. Higher management is a particularly important source of data, because this group will have to reinforce managerial behavior once the program becomes operational and subordinate managers are learning the new skills.

In field tests with higher management, questions on the appropriateness of the critical steps and the credibility of the model manager should be emphasized. Conduct the field-test session as a management briefing, rather than as a complete workshop. This briefing should begin with an explanation that the modules have been developed to prototype stage and are currently being field tested. Emphasis should be placed on the importance of having upper management analyze the critical steps and determine whether they would help subordinate managers to be more effective.

Next, the content of the module should be introduced and the introductory material completely reviewed. The setting of the modeling display should be explained and then demonstrated. The discussion of the modeling film should be conducted as a typical management briefing. Two members of higher management should be asked to use the critical steps and simulate a workshop skill practice. The other participants should be asked to discuss the skill practice, focusing on the critical steps. As in the other two types of field test, an observer should record data on an evaluation instrument.

Throughout the entire field test, collect the evaluation instruments from the observers and integrate the data from all the groups. Look for commonality of reaction, both positive and negative, and compare the results with the original task-analysis information.

After you study the feedback on a prototype you have produced, decisions to change critical steps, the model's behavior, and the setting rest solely with you. These may be difficult decisions. As a rule of thumb, however, make changes when more than half the reactions indicate a change is warranted. This does not mean that the recommended behaviors must be adopted, but the recommended behaviors should be compared for effectiveness and compatibility with the program objectives, the generic skills, and the review of the literature. Appropriate revisions can then be made.

If the field test results in relatively minor changes, you are ready to produce the final modeling display. If, however, the field test indicates major changes, you may need to rewrite the script outline or the script or select different talent, as well as schedule another field test for the new modeling display.

6. Final Modeling Display

In most cases, the field-test data will call for revisions in the script or the critical steps. The script may require drastic revisions—perhaps an entirely different manager dealing with a new problem situation. On the other hand, the revised script may be very similar to the prototype.

After revision, run through one or more readings to finalize the script. Enlist skillful managers or instructors to read through the script as the model manager and subordinate to make sure the script flows smoothly and is understandable. When the script is finalized, determine the medium for the final modeling display. Three criteria should be considered: classroom audiovisual equipment, impact, and production costs.

Classroom Audiovisual Equipment. Survey the equipment available in the classrooms. Although both color-videotape and motion-picture equipment are available in many organizations, one or the other may be more easily accessible to the instructors who will conduct the training. For example, if most of the training is to take place in the field, it may be considerably more convenient and less expensive for instructors to carry a 16-millimeter projector than to carry or rent videotape equipment.

Impact. To a certain point, the larger the screen, the greater the impact. Therefore, select a medium that allows projection onto a large screen, such as color motion picture or large-screen video. It is essential for all participants to see clearly all the nonverbal behavior.

Production Costs. Production costs can vary greatly for both film and videotape, depending on the number of cameras used and whether the production takes place in a studio or on location. Several other factors also influence production costs, including the number of actors, the length of production, the number of scenes, the complexity of the sound effects, and the amount of motion (physical activity) in the film.

The process for planning the shooting schedule and assigning responsibilities is very similar to the process for developing the prototype modeling display. Generally, the final modeling display consists of more—but shorter—scenes than does the prototype, because the esthetic composition of the film or tape is critical. The modeling display must still depict appropriate behaviors, but it must also have some esthetic appeal to the viewer. All the items noted in this section point to a production that takes more—sometimes significantly more—time and money than does the prototype.

A FEW MORE CONSIDERATIONS

Thus far, the main process has been outlined for developing a modeling display. This section details important, specific parts of the process.

Model Characteristics

According to Goldstein and Sorcher (1974), behavior changes significantly more when the model is viewed by the observer as highly competent, knowledgeable, friendly, helpful, having high status, or controlling desired resources. They also state that behavior changes significantly more when the model is of the same sex and race as the observer and when the model is rewarded for using the desired behaviors. In their words, "We are all more likely to model powerful, but pleasant, people who receive reinforcement for what they are doing, especially when the nature of such reinforcement is something we, too, desire" (p. 28).

Goldstein and Sorcher are describing models for managers. Therefore, some of the characteristics they describe, such as controlling desired resources, may not pertain to other situations. However, as a general rule, models should appear competent and friendly and should be rewarded when they display specific behaviors.

Modeling Display Characteristics

Except for Goldstein and Sorcher's work, very little has been published about the characteristics of the modeling display. In their view, modeling displays are most effective when they depict behaviors (a) in a vivid, detailed manner; (b) in rank order, from least to most difficult; (c) with sufficient frequency and repetition to make overlearning probable; (d) with a minimum of irrelevant detail (i.e., without behaviors *not* to be modeled); and (e) by using several different models.

I, also, have found that the modeling display must show behaviors in a vivid and detailed manner, with a minimum of irrelevant detail. The sequencing of the behaviors from least to most difficult is most easily handled when sequencing skill modules in the complete training program. In my experience, the proper sequencing of easy and difficult behaviors is more a function of the placement of the skill modules in a program than a characteristic of the modeling display. For example, a program for supervisors may begin with a module such as "Improving Work Habits," which is fairly easily mastered. It may end with "Conducting a Performance Appraisal," which is a relatively difficult skill module.

Overlearning is a function of skill practice and feedback to the learner, rather than a function of the modeling display. Therefore, as you work on your modeling display, concentrate on developing a film or videotape that is credible and vividly demonstrates the desired behaviors. Then use skill-practice exercises to develop overlearning.

Although ideally you may want to develop several different modeling displays for one skill, they are sometimes impractical because of the expense. In terms of learning, we may receive a greater payoff by developing three separate modeling displays for three separate skills, rather than by developing three modeling displays for the same skill.

Acted Versus Natural Models

Walter (1977) indicates that acted modeling displays are more effective than natural modeling displays in bringing about behavioral change. In acted modeling displays, the actors are asked to use a greater degree of expression and nonverbal behavior than are natural displays. In natural modeling displays, the models act as people do in real life; in acted modeling displays, the talent overemphasize nonverbal behavior and put greater expression into their words. Walter's research indicates that in a problem-solving learning experience, at least, the learners develop more behavioral changes after observing an *acted* modeling display than they do after observing a natural modeling display.

Achievability

The learner must believe that after completing the module, he or she can achieve the skill shown by the model. Modeling displays should depict satisfactory, not exemplary, skill levels, because satisfactory behavior appears to be achievable, whereas exemplary actions will most likely appear to be beyond the capability of the viewer.

Positive and Negative Behaviors

A modeling display should also depict effective, not dysfunctional, behavior. Because learners remember the model's behaviors—including any *inappropriate* behaviors—there is little benefit in portraying dysfunctional behavior. Many times this mental picture can inhibit them from learning the correct behaviors; they usually have enough dysfunctional behaviors in their repertoires without being exposed to new ones. If, for example, a module is designed to develop oral presentation skills, there is no value in showing examples of poor oral presentations. Instead, provide viewers with examples of good oral presentations and use feedback after their skill practice to correct any specific dysfunctional behaviors they demonstrate.

Summary of Characteristics

Modeling displays will have more impact when the behaviors are vivid, when there is a certain amount of repetition, and when they portray a minimum of irrelevant or undesirable behaviors. In addition, the model should be viewed as real and the skills as achievable. The most effective modeling displays contain a vivid portrayal of behaviors that seem real to the viewer and that are displayed with satisfactory rather than exemplary skill.

Which Is Better?

Which is better: scripted or unscripted, professional or nonprofessional talent? Training professionals will always debate whether to develop modeling displays with professional talent and carefully prepared scripts or with nonprofessional talent and no script.[6] Research has not indicated that one approach is more effective than the other. The

---

[6]See, for example, Daniels (1981) and Zemke (1982).

following lists of the characteristics of each may be helpful in making the decision for a particular situation.

Scripted Production with Professional Talent:

1. The scripted production can be more precise, because specific dialog can be inserted in the final product.
2. A prepared script allows more examples of desirable behaviors.
3. The scripted production normally is more succinct.
4. The scripted production results in fewer mistakes, because the talent follow specific lines.
5. The scripted production requires professional talent. The actors must memorize the lines and deliver them on camera in an effective manner. Nonprofessional talent find this task difficult.
6. The scripted production is generally more expensive because of the cost of hiring talent and developing a script.
7. The scripted production normally has a higher success rate. Fewer scripted films or tapes turn out to be unacceptable.

Unscripted Production with Nonprofessional Talent:

1. The unscripted production normally is more flexible. As the actors follow the script outline, they provide more spontaneous behaviors. However, this spontaneity may cause retakes of the same scene to contain considerably different behaviors.
2. The unscripted production normally has fewer examples of desired behavior (i.e., fewer examples of skillful use of the critical steps).
3. The unscripted production normally has more mistakes. There are more situations in which the manager or the employee misspeaks or does not express ideas as clearly or succinctly as the program designer would like.
4. The unscripted production normally uses real managers instead of professional talent. The key is a spontaneous rehearsal by skillful managers, who would follow a script outline. This should be repeated until the program designer retakes each scene several times. These retakes are then combined by using the best portions of each take.
5. Unscripted productions usually require more out-takes—the deletion of footage unacceptable for classroom use—partly because many managers find it difficult to behave naturally while on camera. The out-takes require extra editing time and special skill.

6. The unscripted production is normally less expensive at the front end, because it does not require a script-writing team or professional talent. However, given the usual percentage of out-takes, additional time and costs should be allotted for the later stages of production.

Generic Versus Organization-Specific Modeling Displays

There is no reported difference in the effectiveness of generic versus company-specific modeling displays. A generic display is produced for a wide variety of audiences. It contains a situation that can be used with managers and supervisors in almost every type of industry or organization. The "company-specific" film is produced for a specific organization, and an "industry-specific" film is produced for a specific industry.

The effectiveness of the modeling display does not hinge on whether it is generic or industry/company specific. Any display will be effective if it is understandable to the audience, uses credible models, and is perceived as containing a situation that could have actually happened in real life.

Generic displays have wider applications, because they are not limited to one industry or company. However, the program designer must select a situation that can be understood by a wide audience.

Industry- or company-specific displays have more narrow applications, because each is designed for one company or industry. In some cases, because of regional or divisional differences, their uses may be confined to specific geographic regions or divisions of organizations. Although the production costs are generally the same for generic and specific films or tapes, some savings may result from using free on-location settings for specific displays. For generic productions, a location or studio is often rented. On the other hand, a company- or industry-specific production can become obsolete more quickly, because changes in equipment or policy date certain elements of the modeling display.

COMMENT

When people first use behavior-modeling technology, they tend to emphasize the modeling display over other parts of the learning experience. The reason may be that the modeling display is more fun to develop and is the most visible part of a modeling program. Unfortunately, most programs using behavior modeling are evaluated more on the quality of the modeling display than on the effectiveness of the learning experience. I hope all of us can do something to change this. Although the modeling display is a crucial part of the learning experience, it is useless without the support of the other elements.

The effective modeling display utilizes appropriate critical steps, is well scripted, has a credible model, has good technical quality, and is developed in concert with the other required software. The key is to commit enough resources to the production of the modeling display to make it credible and useful to the viewer. The modeling display can then be used with many learners, thereby greatly increasing its return on investment.

REFERENCES

Daniels, W.R. How to make and evaluate video models. *Training and Development Journal,* 1981, *35*(12), 31-33.

Goldstein, A.P., & Sorcher, M.A. *Changing supervisor behavior.* Elmsford, NY: Pergamon Press, 1974.

Walter G.A. Acted vs. natural models for performance oriented behavior change in task groups. *Journal of Applied Psychology,* 1977, *16*(3), 303-307.

Zemke, R. Building behavior models that work. *Training,* 1972, *19*(1), 22-27.

5

Neglected Software:
The Skill-Practice Exercise

Alice Harmon[7], director of management development with the RDT Company, called me one day and said, "Say, Jim, next time you're out my way, I'd like to have you stop in and take a look at the middle-management program I just purchased. It uses behavior modeling and teaches managers to develop interactive skills in the areas of problem analysis, decision making, and planning."

Three weeks later, I spent an afternoon with Alice, examining the new program. We looked at the critical steps and, in general, I found them satisfactory. We also examined the modeling displays and they were quite good.

Then I asked Alice, "What about the skill-practice material?"

Her response was "I don't know; I haven't even looked at it!"

"Red alert," I thought to myself. "If the skill practices are weak or poorly designed, Alice could really have some problems."

I decided it would be unwise to express my concern at this time. After all, Alice had bought the program from a competitor; if I were critical of it, she might think professional jealousy prompted my comments. In addition, I had not seen the skill-practice materials and I did not want to bias her negatively prior to their use.

I asked Alice why she had purchased the program without looking at the skill-practice activities. Her response was "I liked the films."

Several months later I had a chance to chat with Alice on the telephone. Near the end of our conversation, I asked how her new program for middle managers was going. She said they had some trouble getting it started, but it was going great. She had to redo all the skill-practice exercises. The managers had found them confusing, and in a lot of cases there were insufficient data. In fact, they spent twenty-two days of staff time modifying those skill practices. She added that the modification was both unexpected and costly.

---

[7]Alice Harmon is a composite of various people with whom the author has been associated.

Alice Harmon's situation is not unusual. I have found that many training professionals do not examine the skill-practice materials when they purchase behavior-modeling programs. This is unfortunate because most of the learners' classroom time is spent in skill-practice exercises. Recall what takes place in a skill module: The instructor first presents the instructional objectives (the critical steps), and then the participants view and discuss the modeling display. The remainder of the skill module—about 80 percent of the time in the classroom—consists of skill practice and feedback.

Skill-practice exercises are often neglected during the purchase or development of the program. However, once the skill practice begins in the classroom, poorly designed skill-practice exercises become sorely apparent and eventually have to be changed.

Any answer to *why* skill-practice exercises are commonly neglected during the purchase or development of a behavior-modeling program is speculative, because there is a lack of published research concerning this subject. Nevertheless, of all the software in a behavior-modeling program, the skill-practice exercise is the least conspicuous, least glamorous, and least exciting. It requires a lot of meticulous, hard work to develop. Writing a skill-practice exercise is not nearly as much fun as producing a modeling display.

WHAT SHOULD A SKILL PRACTICE DO?

The skill-practice segment of the module is designed to accomplish eight main objectives.

1. Develop Skills. The primary objective of the skill practice is to help participants develop the desired skills. A well-designed exercise must establish a situation and provide enough information for the participants to develop their skills through a success experience.

2. Develop Confidence. The second objective is to develop confidence to the extent that participants will attempt to handle similar situations in real life. Therefore, the skill-practice situation must seem realistic and be just as difficult as those faced in real life. After handling a realistic, yet difficult, situation in the classroom, participants will be more likely to feel confident that they can handle real-life situations.

3. Offer a Variety of Situations. The skill practices need to offer a variety of situations similar to those the learners will confront in real life. For example, if the skill is "introducing change," the exercises must provide opportunities to introduce various types of change and to experience various kinds of reactions by those people affected by the changes.

4. Provide Success Experiences. Skills are developed through a series of skill practices handled successfully. If the learners experience success, they are able to analyze the exercises more objectively and provide meaningful feedback. Success provides the confidence required to handle even more difficult situations in future skill practices. Skill-practice exercises must be designed to provide a series of successes through increasingly difficult situations.

5. Provide Challenge. An exercise without challenge becomes redundant and boring. It must provide sufficient challenge to stimulate participants to prepare for the exercise, to do their best during the exercise, and to feel it was worthwhile.

6. Offer Real-Life Situations. Learners must feel that the skill-practice situation is typical of real life. If it seems artificial, learning will be reduced.

7. Solve Problems. Many skill practices are designed to help participants learn to solve or prevent problems. They are based on the concept that if the learners follow the critical steps and use the given data, they will be able to solve or prevent problems. This means that an exercise must contain complete and sufficiently relevant data to enable the learners to solve problems.

8. Provide Opportunities for Learner-Generated Situations. Many learners will be concerned with situations they must handle back on the job and will want to practice handling them in the classroom. Therefore, the skill-practice segment of the module must give learners opportunities to examine their own situations on the job, select pertinent data, and put those data in a workable format for skill practice.

THE EFFECTS OF NEGLECT

We can legitimately ask, "So what?" If we have appropriate critical steps and good modeling displays, so what if the skill-practice exercises are not as complete and polished as some people might desire? Here are a few examples of what can happen when the exercises are not well designed.

1. Lack of Challenge. Exercises that are too easy do not challenge the participants and can give them false confidence. They may feel they can readily handle real situations, whereas they are practicing with situations that are considerably simpler than those they will face in real life.

Also, participants who realize that the skill practices are too easy to tax their capabilities quickly lose interest. If skill practices are not challenging, they can become dull and redundant. Participants may become bored with the learning experience and may ask, "Why don't we just talk about these issues rather than skill practice them?" or "Why don't you get some skill practices that pertain to our organization?"

2. Win-Lose Situations. Another common problem is setting up a win-lose situation. Effective skill practices in behavior modeling programs allow for win-win solutions. If either party in the skill practice has considerably more power (such as more information or resources), that person can use that power to win at the expense of the other. The win-lose solution teaches that the best way to handle a situation is to win at the expense of the other person. This is particularly dangerous because many times neither the participants nor the instructors realize that the skill practice has set up a dysfunctional learning experience.

3. Insufficient Information. A poorly designed skill-practice exercise may lack some piece of information needed to resolve the situation. Each role player will then create data—typically data that will provide himself or herself with a distinct advantage. This results in a win-lose situation with all its inherent disadvantages.

4. Confusing Information. Poorly designed skill practices can be confusing. The background information may be inconsistent. For example, in a module on handling employee complaints, the subordinate's information sheet might state that he or she had mentioned the situation to the supervisor once or twice before, whereas the supervisor's information sheet inadvertently omits any reference to previous comments. This discrepancy could result in a confrontation during the skill practice, in which the employee would say, "I've mentioned this to you before," and the supervisor would answer, "No, you haven't." The resulting disagreement during the skill practice may produce behavior that is inappropriate for the critical steps of the skill module. After the activity, the role players would compare their information sheets and discover the discrepancy.

The net result of inconsistent background information is confusion during the skill practice and a discussion afterward about those areas in which the data were inconsistent, both of which inhibit the learning process.

5. Too Difficult. It is easy to make skill-practice exercises too difficult. After seeing the modeling display and attempting to follow the critical steps, the learners may discover that the problem is too difficult to solve. They may not have the skills necessary to handle such a complex situation. Such a learning experience can be a disaster, because the learner may decide that he or she can never master the skill—an effect that has been labeled "learned helplessness."

Suppose, for example, that managers who are learning to negotiate performance goals with subordinate managers have reviewed and discussed the critical steps and the modeling display. Suppose further that the first skill practice is too difficult for the managers to handle successfully and the experience becomes a *failure* rather than a *success*. Under those circumstances, all the learners in the class might decide that the kind of situation presented in the skill practice could not be successfully handled in the real world by using the critical steps. In other words, they would *learn* that using the critical steps in negotiating performance goals would result in failure. They would see no value in using those critical steps. Furthermore, they would avoid negotiating goals on the job and would instead use some other behavior, such as dictating the goals.

Any of these five deficiencies in skill-practice exercises can inhibit the learning process. They can cause false confidence, lost interest, and confusion and can promote a win-lose approach and learned helplessness. As though those were not enough, they also waste time as the learners discuss what went wrong in the skill practice. Sooner or later, poorly designed exercises must be redesigned or discarded.

GUIDELINES FOR DEVELOPING SKILL PRACTICES

As you develop or select skill-practice exercises, you may wonder whether the final product will be effective. What criteria should you use during the development process? What guidelines should you use to evaluate the activities during the field tests?

If the nine criteria that follow are used during development and field testing, the main objectives of the skill practice will be accomplished.

Data

The data for the skill practice must be logical, consistent, and succinct. The background data must contain sufficient detail for the participants to handle the situation satisfactorily if they follow the critical steps and must be understandable to the target audience. A consistent format enables participants to process the data more quickly, because after a few skill practices, they know where to look for information. Succinct data are also more easily understood. Because a percentage of the target audience will probably be unfamiliar with the setting, the final, written data should be in a simple format.

Issues

The issues with which the skill practice deals must be outlined clearly enough for all learners to understand them. In addition, those who practice the skills should be given individualized information so they can handle their particular roles.

Balance

Because skill building thrives on experiences of success, skill practices should be designed as win-win situations. If the supervisor, for example, has the advantage of power or authority, the employee needs a compensating factor such as a legitimate complaint or several years of above-satisfactory performance. This combination balances the skill practice so that neither person has an unfair advantage. If the supervisor follows the critical steps, he or she should be able to handle the situation successfully. Balance also provides for a sense of reality in the skill practice so that the participants do not feel that they were set up for either an easy success or a harsh failure.

Sufficient Background Information

All participants need sufficient information about the environment to enable them to see the practice situation in context. Typically, this information consists of the titles and responsibilities of the skill-practice participants and a description of the organization. For each role, the following data are needed: a summary of previous discussions, job-performance record, number of years in present position, number of years with the organization, and length of time in the reporting relationship. These data can be supplemented with information about the work unit, including its objectives, responsibilities, and its position in the organization.

Obviously, more background information may be needed, depending on the particular skill. The key is to make sure all learners, including the observers, have sufficient background information to understand the issues and situation in context.

Cultural Acceptability

Strive for realism, avoid stereotyping. To achieve realism, the skill practice must be developed so learners perceive the situation as one that could occur in their culture. Even though a country may use English as its primary language, skill-practice situations may have to be adapted to the particular culture. For example, transportation problems mentioned in a skill practice in the United States may focus on the lack of good public transportation and overcrowded highways. In the United Kingdom, the reference might be to commuter trains that run late. In Australia, the transportation problems may focus on the lack of modern multilane expressways. The language must also be adapted to the terminology of the country or region. In the United States, we would talk about the hood and the trunk of a car, whereas, in the United Kingdom, the terminology would be the bonnet and the boot of the auto.

Stereotyping and the reinforcing of stereotypes must be avoided. Although it is appropriate to use background information that is normal for a particular cultural group, the data must be perceived as descriptive of individual characters in the skill-practice situation. If stereotyping is a problem, the exercises should be reviewed by people who are very familiar with the norms of the characters portrayed in the skill practice.

Specificity

The skill-practice exercise should be specific in terms of dates, times, rates, outputs, and so on, e.g., something happened *six* weeks ago, not a *few* weeks ago. Vague information will produce only confusion in the skill practice.

Reading Level

The reading level should be adjusted to the target audience, although generally, material written at an eighth-grade reading level is appropriate.

Avoidance of Distracting Issues

A distracting issue is any feature of the exercise that is perceived by some learners as comical, critical of people or products, or biased. Therefore, comical names, the names of specific products, and any information that seems to be biased against any group should be avoided.

Obsolescence

Specific data can quickly become obsolete. Therefore, dates should be expressed with the day and month only. References to cultural fads or to specific model numbers and product numbers should be avoided. If the skill practice deals with a product, it should be described in general—not specific or detailed—terms.

DEVELOPING THE SKILL-PRACTICE EXERCISE

The process for developing skill-practice exercises is outlined in Figure 8. By using these seven steps, you can develop skill-practice exercises that will avoid the problems previously mentioned and that will include all the necessary features. Given the behaviors to be enacted in the modeling displays, the task at hand is to design skill-practice exercises that will allow the learners sufficient opportunities to develop the target skills in the classroom.

1. Conduct a critical-incident analysis. The purpose of the *critical-incident analysis* is to obtain data about the issues, environment, and target audience. Data are needed on typical problems, issues frequently encountered on the job, situations that occur in the work environment, work norms and jargon, who handles the problems, where the problems occur, and which problems are not presently being solved.

The source of these data will be those people who encounter the situation being studied. For example, if you were concerned with developing interpersonal skills for airline-reservation clerks, you would collect data from airline-reservation personnel, their managers, travel agencies, and customers who interact with airline-reservation clerks.

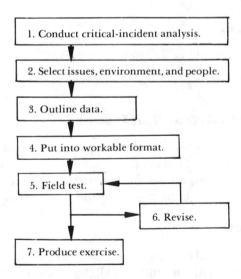

Figure 8. Flow Chart for Developing Skill-Practice Exercises

In doing the critical-incident analysis, the one-on-one interview is most often used. Interviewers typically use a *patterned interview*, a check list of questions to determine whether they have collected all the needed information. A sample patterned interview is shown in Appendix A.

Precise details about each situation are necessary. For example, if you were collecting information about how airline-reservation clerks handle customer complaints, you would ask customers, travel agents, and the clerks' managers to recall specific instances in which clerks handled complaints and to relate the details of each event. You would ask them what led to the situation, what specific dialog transpired, and what, if anything, happened afterward. Not only would you collect data about what happened, but you would also ask for the interviewee's perception of why it happened. Collecting this information from everyone involved is not always possible, because some of the people may not be available or may not want to talk about the incident. In certain customer-contact situations, it may be impossible to identify or locate the second person. Despite these problems, your *goal* should be to talk to all people involved in the interaction. This approach should provide the perceptions of each person before, during, and after the incident.

The critical-incident analysis should continue until you have sufficient data to develop the required number and variety of skill practices. A good rule of thumb is to collect two critical-incident situations for each exercise you are writing.

2. Select issues, environment, and people. In selecting the situations from the critical-incident data, look at the issues involved, the environment, and the people. In other words, as you encounter the various critical incidents, select situations that center on issues most pertinent to the target skill. Your goal at this stage is to establish an environment that is familiar to the audience and to select characters for that environment who are similar to the audience. This part of the process consists of selecting (a) issues that are challenging yet relevant to both the audience and the skill; (b) an environment that is realistic and understandable to the participants; and (c) characters who are similar to the target audience.

3. Outline the data. The specific data needed by each participant should be listed. For example, if the situation portrays a supervisor's interaction with a subordinate, outline the data needed by the supervisor, the subordinate, and the observers. Figure 9, a sample data-base matrix, illustrates a practical method for outlining the data.

4. Put into a workable format. The relevant data in the outline must be translated into a format that can be used in the classroom. Sometimes this format is a narrative description of the situation. The data also can

CRITICAL STEPS FOR SUPERVISOR	DATA FOR SUPERVISOR	DATA FOR SUBORDINATE	DATA FOR OBSERVERS
1. Describe in detail the poor work habit you have observed.	Last two weeks subordinate spent long periods on personal phone calls.	Each day sister calls you at work one or two times. Each call is about 15 minutes.	Supervisor manages accounting department of store chain. Eight clerks match purchase orders to invoices and make payment to suppliers. Clerks spend substantial time on telephone. One subordinate, a clerk for 5 years, does satisfactory work, has good relations with the stores and suppliers, but spends long periods of time on personal phone calls. Telephones are used for business; personal calls are limited to 3 minutes.
2. Indicate why it concerns you.	Telephones are used for business and must be available for outgoing and incoming calls. Personal phone calls are discouraged.		
3. Ask for reasons and listen openly to the explanation.		Younger sister just separated from husband; has two pre-school children; taking separation very hard; depends on you.	
4. Indicate that the situation must be changed and ask for ideas for solving the problem.	Phones to be used for business; personal calls limited to 3 minutes.		
5. Discuss each idea and offer your help.	Subordinate can call when not at work.	You can call during break and at lunch. "Emergency calls" must be accepted.	
6. Agree on specific action to be taken and set a specific follow-up date.			

Figure 9. Sample Data-Base Matrix: Improving Poor Work Habits

be presented through tables, graphs, or facsimiles of letters and memos. The key is to determine what format will best enable the participants to absorb the information quickly and allow them to refer to it and make appropriate notes during the skill practice.

5. Field test the exercise. Once a skill practice has been put into a workable format, the next step is the field test, which generally is presented as a regular learning experience, rather than as an experiment. An *error analysis* can help determine areas in which the exercises are deficient. An observer can record "errors" by the participants during the field-test skill practice.

6. Revise the exercise. The parts of the exercise that caused problems must be changed. Parts of the exercise may be inconsistent, too simple, or too difficult; they may lack a win-win balance; or they may not provide sufficient information.

After the revisions, field test the exercise again. When it passes the field test with flying colors (i.e., when participants use the critical steps effectively), move to the production stage.

7. Produce the exercise. When the field tests are completed and the activity is in its final form, the necessary number of copies may be reproduced.

LEARNER-GENERATED SKILL PRACTICES

The ultimate purpose of skill-practice exercises is to build skill and confidence in the learners, to provide them with success experiences in multiple situations, and to give them the ability to transfer the skill from the classroom to the job. To fully meet these objectives, the role of the skill practice changes toward the end of the learning experience.

The initial skill-practice exercises in a module should provide success experiences in a nonthreatening environment. This is most easily and efficiently accomplished with previously prepared skill practices, which have the advantage of presenting clear-cut issues in win-win situations. In addition, the degree of challenge and the required quantity and type of coaching can be determined in advance. One of the big advantages of instructor-provided skill practices is that they can be designed neither to impede the learning process nor to contain distracting elements. Also, the instructor-provided skill practice can be field tested for effectiveness.

As the learners become more skilled and confident, they move to a greater proportion of learner-generated skill practices, which deal with situations the participants will face on the job. When participants successfully handle their own situations in skill practices, they develop the confidence to handle similar situations on the job.

The same criteria pertain to learner-generated skill practices: The data must be specific, the issues must be clearly described, there must be sufficient background information, and so on. Nevertheless, there are two main requirements for creating successful learner-generated skill practices:

1. A well-designed format in which the authors (the learners) are cued on the specific information needed (e.g., date and time of discussion or percent of sales budget attained in first three months). Samples of formats are given in Figures 10 and 11.

2. Instructor coaching to help the authors enter all information needed on the form in a clear, succinct manner. The authors should write the subordinate's information from the subordinate's point of view.

Learning seems to be most effective when prepared skill practices are used immediately after the learners view the modeling display, and learner-generated skill practices are more effectively used later in the module. For example, in a class of six supervisors, you could use three prepared skill practices followed by three learner-generated exercises in each of the first four or five modules. In later modules, the ratio could be one or two prepared activities followed by four or five created by the learners.

SUMMARY

Skill and confidence cannot be built without effective skill practices. Poorly designed skill practices can confuse learners, cause them to lose interest, or give them a false sense of confidence. They can also imply that the win-lose approach is best or, even worse, promote learned helplessness. Well-designed skill practices can add excitement and challenge to the classroom and give a feeling of success as participants use the skills in real-life situations.

MANAGER'S INFORMATION

Describe your own situation.

MANAGER _____ , _____
                NAME (real or fictitious)   JOB TITLE

SUBORDINATE _____ , _____
                NAME (real or fictitious)   JOB TITLE

Work setting:_____

Situation to be discussed: _____

_____

Previous discussions (relevant to this situation): _____

_____

Other important facts about the situation: _____

_____

Manager's objectives during discussion: _____

_____

Important information about:	Manager	Subordinate
Years of service with organization	_____	_____
Years in this position	_____	_____
Years reporting to this manager		_____

Subordinate's normal performance: satisfactory or unsatisfactory (circle one)

Subordinate's general attitude about his or her job: _____

_____

NOTE: Before starting the skill-practice exercise, the participant who portrays the manager should have time to study the work sheet and to prepare for the discussion.

_____

                        YOUR NAME

**Figure 10. Sample Format for Learner-Generated
Skill Practice: Manager's Form**

SUBORDINATE'S INFORMATION

Describe your own situation.

SUBORDINATE _____ , _____
NAME (real or fictitious)   JOB TITLE

MANAGER _____ , _____
NAME (real or fictitious)   JOB TITLE

Work setting: _____

Subordinate's information about situation to be discussed: _____

_____

_____

Subordinate's responses to supervisor's description of situation: _____

1. _____

2. _____

3. _____

Subordinate's general attitude about the situation: _____

_____

Important information about:	Manager	Subordinate
Years of service with organization	_____	_____
Years in this position	_____	_____
Years reporting to this manager		_____

Subordinate's normal performance: satisfactory or unsatisfactory (circle one)

Subordinate's general attitude about his or her job: _____

_____

NOTE: Before starting the skill-practice exercise, the participant who portrays the subordinate should have time to study the work sheet and to prepare for the discussion.

_____

YOUR NAME

**Figure 11. Sample Format for Learner-Generated
Skill Practice: Subordinate's Form**

6

Getting the Most
out of the Modeling Display

The instructor—let us call him Dave Templeton—had shown a modeling display to a group of managers from retail stores. The managers began to discuss the best way to determine which employees should work evenings. Some managers said the decision should be made solely by the retail-store manager. Others felt the employees as a group should decide, and still others said the department managers should decide.

Dave's problem was that the managers' discussion began to focus on how they scheduled employees' time in their own stores and to veer away from their objective, to develop the skill "overcoming resistance to change." Although the managers had viewed the display just twenty minutes earlier, they had not caught the significant behaviors used by the model manager. They did notice that he seemed uncomfortable during the first part of the discussion—and they were critical of that— but they completely missed how he had turned the situation around by suggesting that he and his subordinate brainstorm possible solutions. In fact, they had failed to identify much of the significant behavior in the modeling display.

As a result, their discussion of the film centered on peripheral issues. If Dave had properly managed the viewing, the managers could have identified the behaviors that were effective in handling the situation and would have understood the rationale for using those behaviors.

This chapter discusses what you—or Dave Templeton—can do to maximize learning from the modeling display.

THE CONTENT OVERVIEW

In the overall sequence of events in a skill module, the modeling display should be preceded by a content overview describing the need for the skill, the benefits of using the skill, and the critical steps. This overview normally takes no more than ten minutes.

In highlighting the need for the skill, refer to your needs-analysis data. Tell the participants that managers frequently encounter situations requiring that particular skill and that it is a skill for which managers have indicated a need. Relate specific benefits of using the skill on the job. The discussion enables you to check the participants' concerns and understanding of the content.

Describe and discuss effective behavior for each critical step. Provide narrative illustrations to give the participants vivid impressions of the behaviors. For example, in a module on discussing poor work habits with a subordinate, a typical critical step is "Indicate why the poor work habit is of concern to you." To help illustrate the point, you might say, "In this critical step, tell the employee clearly and concisely what your concerns are. You may feel that the poor work habit is potentially dangerous. Perhaps the poor work habit is wasting time, and, therefore, you—as supervisor—cannot achieve your production goals as easily. Perhaps a poor work habit has been observed by other employees, who are complaining about it."

THE MODELING DISPLAY

The main objectives for viewing a modeling display are to identify behaviors that were effective in handling the situation and to understand the reasons for using those behaviors. Three distinct steps, which build one on the other, are required to maximize learning during this segment of the skill module: establishing the context, viewing the modeling display, and identifying significant behaviors (see Figure 12). It usually takes twenty to twenty-five minutes to handle these three steps.

Establishing the Context

In establishing the context, the instructor should first describe the setting and the situation. If, for example, the skill is "handling customer complaints," the instructor might describe the setting as the appliance department of a chain of retail stores. He might explain that Mrs. Bradshaw, who purchased a washer two weeks earlier, would be lodging a complaint with an appliance salesperson, Bill Scofield: The machine had flooded her laundry room on this particular morning.

The next step is to cue the participants to observe specific events that will take place in the display. To continue the example above, the instructor would ask the learners to observe how Bill Scofield responds to Mrs. Bradshaw when she says, "I don't want anything but a new machine. I've had that machine two weeks. I've only put a down

A. (Instructor) Establish context.

   1. Describe setting and situation.

   2. Cue participants.

   3. Give positive introduction.

   4. Stress taking notes.

B. (Participants) View modeling display.

   1. Observe behavior.

   2. Take notes.

C. (Instructor, interacting with participants)
Identify significant behaviors.

   1. Discuss significant behaviors by critical step.

   2. Reinforce taking complete, accurate notes.

   3. Acknowledge alternatives.

   4. Check for understanding.

Figure 12. Maximizing Learning from the Modeling Display

payment on it, so no more money until I get a new machine." This would alert the learners to watch for and listen to Bill's response.

The modeling display should then be introduced in a positive manner, with a brief reference to the relevance of the situation for the participants and a mention of the effectiveness of the model. The instructor might ask the participants to watch the way Bill handles a situation that they encounter almost daily in their jobs and to notice how he shows an understanding of the customer's frustration while reaching an agreement on how to correct the problem.

Just before viewing the modeling display, the importance of taking complete notes should be stressed. Even if note taking has already been mentioned, it is essential to remind the learners at this point to take complete notes for each modeling display as a basis for the discussion of the film and for feedback after the skill practices.

Viewing the Modeling Display

For the participants to receive the most from the modeling display, they must do two things simultaneously: observe behavior and take notes. Each participant is expected to observe the behavior of everyone in the display, paying particular attention to how the model handles the situation, and to record key words and phrases. If participants express difficulty in trying to write while watching the screen, they should be encouraged to use whatever note-taking techniques are easiest for them and assured that watching and writing effective notes will become easier with practice.

Identifying Significant Behaviors

The third step in learning from the display begins after the viewing, when participants try to identify significant behaviors. The participants should be encouraged to describe the model's effective behavior in each critical step. The goal here is to make sure all participants discern the model's behavior that led to the successful handling of the situation and understand why that behavior was effective.

For example, if you had presented a film on handling employee complaints and were about to discuss the critical step "Present your position openly," you might ask what the supervisor did when he presented his position. If you are given an example of significant behavior, thank the participant and clarify why that behavior was effective. This can be done by asking the group or simply commenting on the rationale for handling the critical step in that manner. Then move on to the next critical step. If by chance you do not get an example of significant behavior, then ask other participants if they can supply you with more information. If nobody has accurate or adequate information, provide it and move on to the next critical step.

During the discussion, the instructor should deliberately reinforce complete and accurate note taking. For example, if a learner provides a complete dialog for a significant behavior, the instructor should acknowledge the accuracy of his or her notes.

Be prepared to accept *alternative positive behaviors*. With regard to handling customer complaints, for example, a participant may say, "When I receive a complaint about a new appliance, I always assure the customer that the appliance is under full warranty. In fact, I keep copies of warranties handy, and I show the customer what the warranty says. I didn't see Bill Scofield do that."

If a participant suggests an acceptable alternative behavior, acknowledge that it could improve the handling of the situation and suggest that the alternative be tried in a skill practice. By testing different approaches, participants can examine innovative ways of handling situations and check those methods during the skill practices. Accepting alternatives from participants is an effective way to adapt the modeling display to their real-world situations.

If a suggested alternative behavior conflicts with the behavior being learned in the module, indicate what the conflict is. Participants may still like to try that approach in a skill practice to discover for themselves whether or not it is effective.

After discussing the model's behavior, check with the group to make sure each person understands the behaviors needed to handle the situation and the rationale for using them. This is merely a check for understanding, not an attempt to promote further discussion. Your check may consist of only a question such as "Does anyone have any questions or concerns about the way Bill Scofield handled the situation with Mrs. Bradshaw or about any of the items we discussed after the film?"

Respond immediately to any questions or concerns raised. Questions often focus on why the model handled the situation in a particular manner. In response, explain how that behavior supports a particular critical step or the generic skills covered in the program. Concerns normally center on whether or not the behavior demonstrated by the model supervisor is appropriate for the learner's organization. When this occurs, turn the question back to the group to see how the others feel. If the consensus is that the behavior is appropriate, then move on to the skill practice. If the consensus is that the behavior may not be appropriate, suggest a test of that behavior in learner-originated skill practices. In this way, the participants can test the behavior in a situation that is closer to reality for their organization.

AN EXAMPLE: THE C&T COMPANY

In the following illustration of how an instructor puts the process into action, instructor Joyce Iverson works with a group of six first-line supervisors in a skill module on "overcoming resistance to change."

The C&T Company manufactures refuse-collection equipment. The six supervisors in Joyce Iverson's classroom oversee the production and assembly of refuse compactors and containers, which are then mounted on truck chassis. The work requires highly skilled employees who can produce a high quality product that meets the buyer's specifications.

Content Overview

During the content overview, Joyce establishes the need for the skill "overcoming resistance to change" and highlights the benefits of using it on the job. In establishing the need, she refers to the needs-analysis information that had been obtained from the supervisors, their managers, and a sampling of subordinates:

> *In preparing for this workshop, I collected information about your needs as supervisors. Many of you may remember the yellow form you*

filled out and returned to me. In addition, I received information about training needs from your managers. I also interviewed twenty employees to find out what they felt their supervisors were doing well and how they thought you, as supervisors, could be more effective.

These data from you, your managers, and some of your employees suggest that change is a constant factor in everyone's job here at C&T. How do changes required on the job come about? Well, some result from changes in our markets and from our customers' requests for better, more reliable, and more productive equipment. Some are imposed by government in the form of regulations on matters such as occupational safety and health. Other changes are required as a result of union negotiations and changes in organizational policy.

As supervisors, you are an important part in this change process. You communicate changes and implement them within the employee group. Many of you have said that your employees tend to resist change and that you wish you could find some way to reduce this resistance. On the other hand, many of the employees I interviewed believe that management often introduces change in an impersonal manner.

Therefore, this module on overcoming resistance to change will benefit both you and your employees. It will enable you to become more effective in introducing change to your work groups, and your increased skill will help make your employees feel that you are concerned about their reactions when you introduce change.

Joyce adds that the type of change covered in this module is on-the-job change dictated by higher management. As an example, she reminds the supervisors that within the last two months they had been required to implement an important change that involved staggering work hours for all assembly workers. When such a change is dictated, there is no debate about whether it should be implemented; it is a matter of the supervisor's responsibility to implement it in a way that will cause minimum resistance. Joyce points out that this type of change often affects front-line supervisors, particularly when they must implement changes brought about by government regulations, union contracts, and upper-management decisions.

During the content overview, Joyce checks with the supervisors from time to time to see whether they have any questions about the content and responds to questions and concerns. Joyce then outlines the critical steps for overcoming resistance to change (Figure 13) and describes the behavior for each step.

For Critical Step 2, "Explain how the change will affect the employee," for example, Joyce emphasizes that not only must the

1. Give background information and describe why a change is necessary.
2. Explain how the change will affect the employee.
3. Ask the employee for questions about the change.
4. Listen and respond openly to the employee's questions or comments.
5. Ask the employee for his or her help in making the change work.

Figure 13. Critical Steps for Overcoming Resistance to Change

supervisor give his or her subordinate a precise explanation of what is to be done differently, but this step also requires outlining both the favorable and unfavorable effects of the change from the subordinate's perspective:

> *Critical Step 2 also requires that you briefly describe both the positive and negative effects of the change for the employee. Here's an example: Remember when the prefabrication unit was set up three months ago? There were three favorable effects for the level-II machinists: (1) They would spend more of their time in their primary trade (rather than in setting up and moving materials); (2) they would have longer runs on the same product, so they could work more efficiently; and (3) they would be using the new Bitner equipment. On the other hand, the unfavorable effects were (1) the machinists would be relocated to the new prefab area and would not be working with their former co-workers and (2) there would be less variety in their work. That is essentially what the supervisor of the level-II machinists would have said.*

After describing the behaviors for each critical step, Joyce checks for understanding before moving to the introduction of the modeling display:

> *That's an overview of the critical steps in overcoming resistance to change, which you will see in our film. Do you have any questions about any of the critical steps or the specific things to do under each step?*

Establishing the Context

Joyce's first step in establishing the context for the modeling display is to describe the setting:

> *The film you are about to see involves Burt White, manager of the Northside branch of the Key Bank and Trust Company, and Chris Pittman, the senior teller at the Northside branch, who has worked there for approximately five years.*
>
> *Key Bank and Trust operates a main downtown office plus several outlying branches. The Northside branch is located in the North Gate*

*Shopping Center, servicing a suburban area. Recently, two compet-
ing banks announced that new branches in the area would be open
every evening during the week. Because of this, the Key Bank and
Trust Company has decided to be open to the public from 10 a.m. to 8
p.m. instead of 8:30 till 4. These new hours mean that each employee
at the Northside branch will have to work two or three evenings a
week.*

*Because Chris is a key employee, Burt has decided to discuss the new
hours with her first. He feels that having her support is crucial to
making the change work.*

Joyce proceeds to the next step, cuing the participants about
specific situations that will take place:

*Burt handles several difficult areas in this film. The first occurs in
Critical Step 1, when Burt says that competition is increasing. He
explains that a bank opened nearby two months ago and that a second
bank will be opening next month. Notice how he continues by saying
that those banks will be open evenings and will be more convenient
for customers. Notice also how easy it is for Burt to move into the
subject of Key Bank's changing its hours after giving Chris this
background information.*

*Later, during Critical Step 4, Chris tells Burt about the negative
effects of the new hours on her and her children. Notice how Burt
responds by recognizing her concern and acknowledging that her
children are very important to her. Pay attention to the way he
acknowledges her concerns and still works toward a solution to
the problem.*

*Two or three minutes later in the film, we reach the turning point of
the discussion. Chris has expressed several concerns. Burt asks, "Do
you have any ideas on what you might do?" Chris responds, "No, I'm
confused. I can't think of anything." Burt then says he knows this
change has come as quite a shock to her, but if they brainstorm some
ideas, these may be helpful. Notice how the brainstorming session has
a positive and productive effect on the conversation.*

Joyce completes the third step in establishing the context to
give a positive introduction to the modeling display:

*Many of you have faced situations as difficult as those faced by Burt
White—perhaps even more difficult. You will see, however, that even
though Burt has to cope with some difficult responses from Chris, he
is able to guide the discussion very skillfully to a satisfactory outcome.*

As the supervisors observe the film, it is imperative that they
observe all of Burt's behavior. They must also pay enough
attention to Chris for Burt's actions and reactions to make sense in
the context of the situation. Therefore, Joyce's last step in

preparing the learners for the modeling display is to stress the importance of taking notes as an accurate basis for discussing the model:

> *Be sure to take complete notes on the film. Include as much of both actors' behaviors as possible so we can discuss Burt's actions for each of the critical steps in light of his interaction with Chris.*

View the Modeling Display

Joyce starts the film, "Overcoming Resistance to Change," which was produced from the following script.[8]

Introduction

Burt:	Hi, Chris. I really appreciate your staying a few minutes to talk with me.
Chris:	No problem.
Burt:	Well, here, let's sit here.
Chris:	What did you want to see me about?
Critical Step 1:	*Give background information and describe why a change is necessary.*
Burt:	Chris, I'd like to discuss with you a change that's going to take place here in the office. As you know, we're faced with competition: the bank down the street that moved in a couple of months ago.
Chris:	Mm hmm.
Burt:	And First Trust is going to open a new branch in the Miracle Mall next month. And, as you also know, both banks are going to be open in the evenings. They advertise that the hours are more convenient for their customers. So our management feels that the only way to meet this competition is for us to change the hours here at the office.
Chris:	Oh?

---

[8]Script adapted by permission from *Overcoming Resistance to Change*. Copyright © 1979 by Development Dimensions International. All rights reserved.

Critical Step 2:   *Explain how the change will affect the employee.*

Burt: Yes, and the way this will affect the staff is that the hours that are open to the public will be changed from the present eight-thirty till four to ten a.m. till eight p.m., five days a week.

Chris: Eight?

Burt: Yes, till eight in the evening.

Chris: Five days a week? Oh, wow!

Burt: Chris, I know that this is quite a change, and it's going to cause each of us some problems, and that's one reason I wanted to speak with you first. You've been with the bank five years now and are our most experienced teller, and I need your help in solving some of these problems.

Chris: This really is going to cause problems. I mean babysitting, car pooling, fixing meals. Why, even our social life. When does this change become effective?

Burt: The first of October. And I can appreciate the number of problems you are concerned about, Chris. Perhaps it would help if I outlined the new work schedule. It's a staggered work shift, meaning that on alternate weeks you will work from nine-thirty to six on two days and from noon to eight-thirty on three days. Then the next week it would reverse.

Chris: I see.

Critical Step 3:   *Ask the employee for questions about the change.*

Burt: I'm sure you've got some questions about this change.

Chris: Yes, this comes as quite a shock.

Burt: Well, I'm sure that it does, and it probably raises some concerns in your mind.

Chris: Well, I can't help but feel that the bank hasn't taken the employee into consideration in all this.

Burt: Why do you say that?

Chris: Because it's going to cause some problems.

Burt:	And what problems do you see?
Critical Step 4:	*Listen and respond openly to the employee's questions or comments.*
Chris:	The children. As you know, they're both in elementary school, and during the five years I've been here, I've worked out a pretty nice schedule. They get on the school bus in the morning when I'm leaving for work; they're home at three-thirty; and I get home shortly after four-thirty. And it's worked out very nicely. The ten-year-old can supervise the six-year-old for an hour or so, but now we're talking about five hours. To give him that kind of responsibility just wouldn't be fair. Maybe I can find a sitter, a teenager maybe, but I don't know. I've found in the past that if any emergencies come up, they can be pretty unreliable. And then there's dinner. I wouldn't be home to fix the evening meal. And with my husband on the road so much, I don't know from one week to the next what his schedule's going to be.
Burt:	Chris, I know you're concerned about your children and you certainly want to be sure they're safe and that they do have proper meals.
Chris:	That's right; my children are certainly more important to me than my job.
Burt:	Of course, your children are very important to you, Chris, so let's see what we can do to resolve some of these problems. Really—because of the competition—we have no choice here but to go to the new hours.
Chris:	I certainly understand that; I can appreciate it. I've enjoyed working here. The conditions have been so pleasant and I've enjoyed working with you. But I have to ask, what would be the possibility of my being transferred to another branch?
Burt:	Well, Chris, the other branches are in the same boat that we are. They're all having to go to the new hours. All except, of course, the main office.

Chris:	And the possibility of being transferred to the main office?
Burt:	Well, I looked into that with the thought that possibly it would help some of the employees if they could transfer to the main office. However, I found that, well, the staff at the main office is...they're all very stable. The employees who are there have been there for years. They are all long-service employees and, well, out of fairness to you, I feel that you should know that the possibility of your being transferred to the main office is in the future some three to five years.
Chris:	Three to five years! That's too long. The problem wouldn't exist then; it's now. Couldn't special consideration be given to women with younger children? For example, perhaps the male employees could work in the evenings, or women with older children, or older women.
Burt:	Well, I guess they could, but that really wouldn't be fair to the other employees. Now, I know you feel very strongly about this, but, if the shoe were on the other foot, you really wouldn't like being taken advantage of because you happen not to have small children. So we have to rule this out as a solution.
Chris:	What about seniority? I've been here for five years. Doesn't that count for something?
Burt:	Yes, Chris, you have worked here for five years and you've always done a good job. However, if we were to assign the new hours based on seniority, it would seem unfair to the employees here at the branch. What we have to find is a way to handle these new hours without causing hardship on the employees. So, I guess we'll have to go to the staggered work shift and everyone will have to work evenings every other day. Now, have you got any ideas on what arrangements you can make for your children and their dinner on the evenings you do work?
Chris:	No. I'm really confused. I can't think of anything right now.

Burt:	I know that this has come to you as quite a shock. Maybe it would be helpful if we brainstormed some ideas for a minute.
Chris:	Okay. It may help.
Burt:	What about the possibility of preparing the evening meal in advance, say the night before? Now you'll be getting an hour off at supper time and you do live nearby. So, possibly, you can be at home with the children during dinner.
Chris:	Well, I certainly live close enough. If—when I work evenings—I could go home at five, then I would be with them for that hour; and if I prepared something in advance, I could just put it in the oven or whatever. That would solve one problem. But it still leaves the main problem, you know, of having them there from six to eight-thirty—or maybe even later—unsupervised.
Burt:	I know; when your husband's out of town on a trip, Chris, what if you arrange to have a neighbor or friend look after the children? You know, somebody that they could turn to in case of an emergency.
Chris:	I don't know of anyone right now. Possibly I could find a neighbor whom I can hire to be with the children from the time I leave to come back to work until I get back home again after eight-thirty. I just don't know right now. I'll have to talk that over with my husband.
Burt:	Well, I'm sure you will want to talk it over with Roger, and perhaps the two of you can find somebody who is reliable, somebody who can supervise the children when he's out of town and when you have to work in the evenings.
Chris:	I just can't think of anyone right now. But if Roger and I talk it over, perhaps we can come up with an answer.
Burt:	Well, that sounds like a good way to approach the problem, and perhaps, after the two of you have discussed it, a solution will become apparent.
Chris:	Well, I hope so.

Critical Step 5:   *Ask the employee for his or her help in making the change work.*

Burt: I know that it seems overwhelming right now, Chris, but with the competition getting heavier, the whole thing boils down to the fact that I need your help in making this change work. I've just got to ask for your cooperation on this.

Chris: Sure, I understand. I want to cooperate and to help. I do see some rather large problems, but I'm certainly willing to try to work them out.

Burt: Thanks, Chris. You've always cooperated with me in the past, and I really appreciate your willingness to try now. Chris, if there's anything I can do to help, please let me know.

Chris: I don't know what kind of help you can be right now. Certainly, you have to implement the change in hours, and that's the thing that's causing me great concern.

Burt: Yes, I know. We both know that the change in hours has to be implemented, so why don't you discuss the situation with Roger and see if the problems can be worked out. Let me know what you decide.

Chris: O.K., I will.

Burt: Thanks, Chris, and thanks again for your cooperation. I'll be talking with the rest of the staff tomorrow morning, but I did want to discuss this with you first.

Chris: Well, thanks.

Burt: Sure.

Identify Significant Behaviors

After the supervisors view the film, Joyce leads a discussion of the critical steps in the film for about five minutes. The objective of the discussion is to have the learners identify the significant behaviors used by Burt in each critical step.

Joyce begins by asking Tom about what Burt did during Critical Step 1:

Tom, can you give me the specific language used by Burt as he gave Chris the background information and described why the change in bank hours was necessary?

Tom replies:

My notes indicate that Burt said there would be more competition from the bank that opened a month ago and the new bank opening in Miracle Shopping Mall. Because those banks are going to be open in the evenings, management at his bank decided the only way to meet competition was to make their hours more convenient for customers.

Joyce reinforces only the completeness of Tom's notes, because there were some minor inaccuracies in his account of Burt's background information:

You captured most of the thoughts Burt expressed under Critical Step 1. Your notes are quite complete. Why is it important that Burt provide Chris with this information?

Tom:

So Chris can see why management has decided to change the hours.

Joyce:

That is correct. Now let's look at what happened in Critical Step 2.

During the discussion of Critical Step 2, Mark suggests an alternative positive behavior (APB):

I really think Burt did a poor job of explaining how the changes affect Chris. She thought she would be working five nights a week, whereas in reality she would be working only two or three nights.

Joyce frames her response to encourage Mark's statement of an APB:

Yes, Chris was confused there. Now, what could Burt have done to prevent that confusion?

Mark:

Well, rather than saying that the new hours would be from ten a.m. to eight p.m., he could have said that the branch hours were being changed and that each employee would have to work two or three evenings a week.

Joyce:

That would have clarified the situation. When you do the skill practices later, make sure you are very precise in explaining how the change will affect the employee.

The discussion continues for all the critical steps in a similar fashion. After discussing Critical Step 4, Joyce has an opportunity to provide even more positive reinforcement:

Judy, do your notes indicate what Burt said in Critical Step 5, when he asked Chris for help in making the change work?

Judy:

I believe Burt said, "Chris, I know the situation seems overwhelming, but with the competition getting heavier, I need your help in making this change work. I just have to have your cooperation."

Joyce:

Excellent, Judy. You picked out the most significant behavior, and your notes are very accurate. It's important that Burt ask for her help in making the change work, because he must find out—not just assume—that he has her support.

Joyce's last step in this segment of the module is to check with the learners for understanding—not to promote further discussion, but to resolve any concerns or misunderstandings before proceeding to the skill practices:

Does anyone have any questions about how Burt handled the situation in the film?

No? O.K., let's take a ten-minute break before we go on to the skill practices.

The content overview and the modeling display cover the first two segments of the skill module. In many skill modules, both can be accomplished within a thirty-minute period. This means that describing the behavioral objectives and viewing the modeling display usually take only 15 percent of the time devoted to the whole skill module. It is imperative that both be done well. Doing them well does not mean increasing the amount of time spent on them. Instead, it means handling the content overview quickly and succinctly and describing the critical steps clearly, in behavioral terms. It also means establishing the context, viewing the modeling display, and identifying significant behavior without discussing every behavior demonstrated in the film or digressing to irrelevant topics. Intellectualizing about "what if" does not move the learning process forward.

Listening to the content review, discussing the critical steps, and viewing the modeling display should give the learners a sufficient understanding of the critical steps and effective behaviors to proceed with the skill-practice exercises.

7

Skill Practice and Feedback

The other day, I turned down an offer to fly in a Cessna 152.

The doorbell rang. When I opened the door, my friend Rick Anderson was standing there, obviously excited. In a staccato, three-minute monologue, Rick told me how he had purchased the Cessna, that it was in excellent shape, and that he was going to take it up today for the first time. He wanted me to go along.

"I didn't know you were taking flying lessons, Rick," I said.

"Oh, I'm not!" Rick responded. "But I've read the owner's manual, and I've seen a film on how to fly the 152. It showed how to start the plane, take off, climb out, land, and all of those sorts of things. I fact, I saw the film twice. I even took notes on it.

"I also have the pilot's check list. That gives me step-by-step procedures for each part of the flight—starting the engine, taxiing, and taking off. In fact, Jim, I want you to go with me to help out. I thought you could read off the check list to me. That way I can concentrate on what I have to do to fly the plane."

"Rick, have you ever piloted a plane before?"

"No, but I'm mechanically inclined." Then he repeated, "I've read the owner's manual about the plane, I've seen a film about how to fly the plane, I took very good notes, and I have the pilot's check list."

You can see why I declined Rick's offer.

If Rick Anderson's airplane crashed, we would know the reason: The pilot was untrained and unskillful. However, when managers fail, we often wonder why—particularly when they have been trained in a workshop that included reading about management principles and discussing management issues. The failure of these managers, therefore, would most likely be blamed on their lack of ability rather than on inadequate training.

Fortunately, Rick Anderson is only a figment of my imagination. Legal requirements prevent an improperly trained person from receiving a pilot's license.

Piloting a plane requires a high degree of skill that cannot be achieved by merely reading the step-by-step procedure and watching a film. It requires practice under the guidance of a qualified instructor pilot. Managerial training, however, often lacks such precautions. Many managers who fail do so because they have been inadequately trained. Managers cannot develop interactive skills without an opportunity to practice. They need coaching, skill practice, and feedback from a competent instructor.

One of the precepts given in Chapter 1 was "If you can't practice the skill, you can't develop it." Watching a performance does not qualify the spectator to perform. Learning a skill requires a person to attempt it, to experience what transpires during the attempt, and—in many cases—to use trial-and-error tactics. Both experience and research indicate that in early practice situations the learner is often inept and needs additional practice.

Feedback, also, is essential to skill development. Many times we have seen someone handle a situation inappropriately and, when provided with feedback, that person has said, "Why didn't you tell me this before? I've been doing it that way for years." Skill practice alone may enable us to develop skills, but many times those skills are inappropriate or not developed to their fullest. Feedback from a skillful instructor will enable managers to develop the high degree of skill competency needed to handle their jobs.

WHAT MAKES AN EFFECTIVE SKILL PRACTICE?

You will recall from Chapter 5 that three of the purposes of skill practice are to enable managers to develop interactive skills, to help them develop confidence in their ability to handle interactions with employees on the job, and to provide them with opportunities to use the skills in the classroom before they are required to use them on the job. Just as modeling displays must meet certain criteria, so must skill-practice exercises—if they accomplish our stated purposes. During the program-development stage, exercises that meet the following three criteria should be selected or designed:

1. The skill-practice situation must be perceived as realistic by the learners.
2. The skill-practice problem must be solvable when the participants use the behaviors outlined by the critical steps.
3. The various skill-practice situations must increase in difficulty to provide continual skill development.

In a typical module, six participants engage in three prepared and three learner-originated skill practices. Each skill practice is different and increasingly more difficult than the preceding one. Participants who want or need more skill development can participate in additional learner-originated skill practices.

After participants become familiar with skill practicing, many instructors include only one or two prepared skill practices and ask the learners to plan the others. At least one prepared skill practice should be used to make the transition from viewing the modeling display to practicing the skills that are needed on the job. However, skillful instructors can sense the needs and capabilities of the learners in the classroom and can adjust their designs accordingly.

Preparing the Participants

Another requirement for an effective skill practice is to give the learners adequate preparation so the exercise is a success experience. If the skill practices have been properly selected or developed—that is, if they meet the three criteria previously mentioned—preparing the learners for the exercise becomes a classroom procedure.

The first step is to brief all participants on the setting, the situation, and the issues of the exercise and then to coach them on how to handle the situation. Coaching should include responding to questions and concerns about the skill practice as well as asking questions to determine if the participants understand the skill-practice situation. For example, they should understand the objectives for the discussion and how to handle specific critical steps.

Instructor-Managed Feedback

After the skill practice, the instructor should manage the feedback that the group gives to the individual who took the role of the manager. There are three purposes for this immediate feedback:

1. To reinforce the effective behaviors used by the skill-practice manager.
2. To develop alternative positive behaviors (APBs) for those instances in which the manager's behavior was less than effective.
3. To build confidence so that the manager will continue to develop skills and eagerly take on more difficult situations.

As in other training situations the feedback must be stated in behavioral terms; that is, the language must be descriptive rather than evaluative or judgmental. The instructor may need to manage the feedback process in an active or directive way.

In a typical approach after a skill practice, the instructor would first ask the person who played the subordinate a few direct questions to establish the value of the discussion from that employee's perspective: "Did the manager listen to you?" "Did you feel comfortable?" The manager would then be asked whether he or she felt comfortable during the discussion and whether he or she would change anything in handling the situation in the future.

If the instructor can determine how receptive the manager is to feedback on the less-effective behaviors, it will help in deciding how much of each type of feedback the observers should give. Some people react best with less intensive feedback; strong reinforcement on one or two good points might be more effective in building their confidence.

Before the observers provide feedback, they should be reminded of the ground rules. Typical ground rules for effective feedback would be the following:

1. Address all feedback to the skill-practice manager.
2. Refer to specific and significant dialog from the skill practice.
3. Indicate why that dialog was particularly effective or ineffective.
4. If the dialog was ineffective, provide an APB and the rationale for using the APB.

The feedback should be specific. To reinforce effective behavior, the observer should cite exactly what the manager said or did and why this behavior was effective. To suggest improvements, the observer should mention exactly what the manager said or did and suggest a specific APB and explain why the APB would have been more effective. The instructor can ensure quality feedback by periodically asking questions or making comments to help observers state their feedback in behavioral terms or to elicit the reasons for their comments.

Effective feedback management requires one instructor for six to eight participants. Although many professional trainers agree that instructor-managed feedback is effective, some of them prefer larger classes, in which groups of three or four learners provide feedback to one another.

Nevertheless, several shortcomings of participant-managed feedback outweigh the disadvantages of the smaller class:

Poor-Quality Feedback. When learners manage the feedback process on their own, people who are not yet skilled in the critical steps provide feedback to a person who is also not yet skilled. This is a situation most learning theorists and behavioral scientists would avoid, because no one present can provide the criteria against which the skill-practice manager's performance should be judged. In order to promote skill development, someone in the group must already have mastered the skill or, at least, must be able to recognize the components of skill mastery. Because the learners have not mastered the skill at this stage, the instructor must provide the performance criteria during feedback.

Unwanted Feedback. Poorly managed feedback often results in an overemphasis of negative feedback. Consequently, the manager may become defensive or lose self-esteem. When the feedback is poorly managed, the observers may not check with the skill-practice manager to determine what sort of feedback he or she wants and will accept. Unwanted feedback, particularly when it is critical, may have a negative effect on the manager. The bottom line is that unwanted feedback brings about very little change in behavior.

Unbalanced Feedback. All feedback should include an appropriate balance of positive reinforcement, which increases confidence, and suggestions for APBs, which lower confidence. When this balance is not managed by the instructor, the manager's confidence is likely to drop because of an overabundance of APB suggestions.

Misdirection. If inexperienced observers give feedback to an inexperienced participant, they may misdirect the participant regarding the most effective way of handling the situation. There are a number of ways to handle any situation, not all of which are equally effective. When unskilled observers provide APBs, they may suggest behaviors that are less effective than those portrayed in the skill practice. Therefore feedback management by a skillful instructor will result in a greater change in behavior and the acquisition of more appropriate skills. Also, the participants will develop a higher level of confidence and will be more likely to use the skills on the job.

CONTRACTING

Knowles (1977) states that adults often come to a training program expecting to learn through the *pedagogical* processes typified by their childhood classroom education. Through the instructor's skillful design and management of the training activities, the participants move to a learning experience based on the principles of *andragogy*, the science of adult learning. Therefore, in the early modules of a behavior-modeling program, the participants may expect and want the instructor to manage the learning process. In the later modules, however, the participants will probably want to control more of the learning process.

In behavior-modeling modules, *contracting* is one method that can utilize andragogy, particularly during the skill-practice and feedback segments. For example, before starting a skill practice, the skill-practice manager could contract with the observers for help in improving his or her ability to discipline an employee without lowering the employee's self-esteem. The manager would ask one or two of the observers to watch for and provide specific feedback on instances in the skill practice that indicate that the employee's self-esteem was or was not maintained. Contracting allows the skill-practice manager to receive feedback in any areas he or she desires. Through contracting, the participant exercises control over the learning process.

When contracting is used, the instructor should still manage the feedback process. This will ensure that the observers provide feedback on the points requested by the skill-practice manager and will also ensure quality feedback on overall skill use and eliminate misdirection.

AN EXAMPLE: THE NUCOM CORPORATION

This example illustrates what happens in a classroom as an instructor manages the skill practice and feedback session. In this example, the instructor, Kelley, is conducting the eighth module ("Overcoming Resentment") of a ten-module program. She is preparing the learners for the first skill-practice exercise, and she has been describing the critical steps. Her major points are summarized in the following paragraphs.

Critical Steps for Overcoming Resentment

1. Explain what you have observed and why it concerns you.

As the employee's manager, you must describe the behavior that seems to indicate resentment. Before discussing this with the employee, make notes on specific behaviors that indicate resentment. In the discussion, describe several of these instances. This does *not* mean you should present the employee with a list of poor behaviors. Rather, you should mention these behaviors simply to illustrate why you wanted to talk.

Tell the employee why this behavior concerns you. Presumably, it has had some effect on the productivity of the work group, on the morale of the work group, or on your ability to work effectively with the employee.

2. Ask for reasons and listen attentively.

Before indicating that you interpret the behavior as resentment, ask for reasons for the behavior and listen attentively. (If there is very little response, proceed to Critical Step 3.)

If the employee explains the behavior in terms unrelated to resentment toward the supervisor, switch to the critical steps of an appropriate skill, such as "handling employee complaints."

3. Discuss sources of resentment, including yourself.

Bring up the issue of resentment. Raise the issue objectively, and directly ask if the employee *does* feel resentment. If the employee acknowledges feelings of resentment, discuss the sources of resentment in detail.

If the employee denies any resentment, do not press the issue. He or she may be telling the truth. Thank the employee for listening to you and indicate that you hope those behaviors can be avoided in the future. Ask the employee for suggestions about what can be done to change those behaviors. If the employee seems to be willing to discuss solutions, enter into a problem-solving discussion.

4. Indicate that you understand the employee's feelings.

If the discussion continues, indicate that you understand why the employee may feel resentment. If the employee adds anything to the conversation about his or her feelings, respond empathically.

5. Discuss possible solutions and agree on specific action.

If the conversation has continued through Critical Step 4, a discussion of possible solutions would be beneficial. Although a complete resolution may not be possible at this time, you may want to examine possible alternatives to *reduce* the resentment.

The specific action you agree on may be to have future discussions, to provide the employee with more information, or to take appropriate actions to improve the situation.

6. Indicate your confidence that the situation will improve.

Since this has probably been a very difficult conversation for both you and the employee, end on a positive note. Thank the employee for discussing the problem and express your confidence that the situation will improve.

After discussing the critical steps, Kelley distributes the appropriate background-information sheets for the skill practice to the observers and the participants. These sheets include the following information.

Background Information for Skill Practice

For Observers

The supervisor is an engineering manager for a firm that manufactures electronic components. He (or she, if a female portrays the part) is responsible for plant engineering, which involves monitoring the manufacturing processes and developing new, low cost, high quality manufacturing procedures.

The employee is one of the industrial engineers reporting to the supervisor. She (or he, if a male portrays the part) has been with the company eight years and has a record of good performance. The employee's primary responsibility is developing new procedures that will reduce the cost of manufacturing. For the past three years, she has turned in more cost reductions than any of the other engineers reporting to her supervisor. For the first three months of this year, her cost reductions totaled $250,000.

Three months ago, the supervisor suspended the employee for one week without pay for smoking in a hazardous area. This was a serious violation because (1) the employee had already received a warning for smoking in that area and (2) if the material had ignited, it could have caused a major explosion. Previously, other employees had smoked in the area without being suspended. However, the plant manager had recently stressed that, without exception, the first offense would result in a warning and the second offense would carry a one-week suspension without pay.

Since that suspension, the employee seemed to avoid talking to the supervisor. She has not been keeping the supervisor as well informed about problems in manufacturing as before. She has been sending the supervisor more memoranda and initiating fewer conversations, which had previously been more effective and informative. Furthermore, her cost reductions for the last three months dropped to $125,000—only half the first-quarter figure.

For Supervisor

You are an engineering supervisor for a firm that manufactures electronic components. You are responsible for plant engineering, which involves monitoring the manufacturing processes and developing new, low cost, high quality manufacturing procedures. You supervise seven industrial engineers and three associate engineers. You report to the manager of the engineering division. Although you are involved with manufacturing procedures, the supervisors of the production lines report to the manager of the manufacturing division.

Recently, you began experiencing difficulty with one of your industrial engineers. This employee has been with the company eight years and has been an excellent engineer. Her (or his, if a male portrays the part) primary responsibility is developing new manufacturing procedures that will reduce the cost of manufacturing. For the past three years, she has produced more cost reductions than any of your other industrial engineers. For the first three months of this year, she turned in $250,000 worth of cost reductions. This employee is always very thorough on project reports, and all of her reduction cases have returned the forecast savings.

For the past three months, however, this employee has been acting strangely and has shown substantially fewer cost reductions. She has not been keeping you informed of problems in manufacturing, and often your first source of information about the difficulties is one of the production-line supervisors. In addition, when you and this employee discuss problems, you have to tell her how to handle them, because she no longer volunteers any solutions.

It appears that this behavior was a result of disciplinary action that you had to take against her about three months ago. Two production-line supervisors reported seeing her smoking in a hazardous area. She did not deny the incident. This was a serious offense because (1) this employee had already received a warning for smoking in that area and (2) if the material caught fire, it could result in an explosion that could destroy the entire plant. This problem was further complicated by the fact that a production-line supervisor had just suspended a union steward for smoking in the same area. This suspension almost resulted in a union walkout. Your manager told you at the time of the threatened walkout that if any one of your people was caught smoking in that area, the person was to immediately receive a one-week suspension without pay. If you had let this employee off with just another warning, the shop employees would probably have walked out in protest.

At the time you suspended her, you were so anxious to finish the distasteful task that you really did not give her much explanation. You did not tell her about the union problem or your manager's directive.

You are quite disturbed about her resentful behavior, and you feel you must discuss this problem with her. She is one of the most valuable engineers in your organization, and you are quite interested in gaining her commitment again. You have asked her to come to your office to discuss some projects. Before getting into that discussion, you are going to try to discuss this apparent resentment.

For Employee

You are an industrial engineer for a firm that manufactures electronic components. You are responsible for developing improved manufacturing processes that reduce manufacturing costs. In the first three months of this year, you turned in $250,000 worth of cost reductions. For the past three years, you have turned in more cost reductions than any other engineer.

Then something occurred that took away most of your enthusiasm. Two production-line supervisors reported seeing you smoking in a hazardous area. You had never considered the area to be very dangerous, so when you wanted to smoke, you lit up a cigarette. At the time the supervisors saw you smoking, you were involved in a critical experiment and did not want to interrupt it. Besides, you had been warned once when you were smoking in this area, and nothing more had happened.

However, when your supervisor was told about this incident, he (or she, if a female portrays the part) suspended you for one week without pay. You felt this action was extremely harsh, because others had been caught and only warned. Production-line employees still smoke in that area when their supervisors are not around. When your supervisor took this disciplinary action, he gave you almost no explanation. You were simply told that you had been warned before and that you should have known better.

This suspension occurred three months ago. You already suspected that your supervisor did not like you, and the suspension convinced you that your suspicion was correct. You know that you are a good employee, and you cannot understand this harsh action. Even your supervisor has praised your work during performance reviews and has given you outstanding ratings. In spite of this, you believe that management must not respect you very much. As far as you are concerned, you may as well look for a job where your hard work will be recognized.

Your supervisor has asked you to come to the office to discuss some work assignments.

Kelley had already asked two of the learners to participate in the skill practice. We will refer to the manager as Mark and to the employee as Anna—both in their character roles and in their real-life roles. In real life, Mark is a manager in the new-product-development department of the NuCom Corporation, and Anna is a manager in the marketing department of the same company. The other four learners in the classroom are also managers from those two departments. After everyone has his or her own information sheet, Kelley summarizes the information that is common to all the sheets and sets the stage for the skill practice:

> *In this skill practice, Mark is taking the part of an engineering manager in a firm that manufactures electronic equipment. Anna is taking the part of an industrial engineer reporting to Mark. Three months ago, Mark suspended Anna for a serious work-rule violation, smoking in a hazardous area. Since then, Anna has been behaving in a way that Mark perceives as resentful; mainly, she has avoided talking to him. In addition, the cost reductions she has been accountable for have declined 50 percent during this period.*

Kelley then coaches Mark privately for a few minutes so he can become fully prepared to handle the situation with Anna. She first asks Mark whether he has any questions or concerns about the skill practice. Then she asks three questions, to help her determine how well Mark understands the content of the skill practice:

> *Which of Anna's behaviors suggest that she may feel resentment?*
> *What are some of the possible reasons for Anna's resentment?*

What constraints will you be under during this discussion?

As Mark responds to each question, Kelley clarifies any issues or procedures that do not seem completely clear to Mark. For example, Mark responds to the second question, about possible reasons for Anna's resentment, this way:

Anna is mad at me because I gave her a suspension three months ago.

Kelley knows that there are other factors influencing Anna's behavior, which are mentioned on Anna's fact sheet but not on Mark's. Specifically, Anna believes that Mark does not like her and that the incident leading to the suspension has threatened her career with the company:

That is probably one reason for Anna's resentment, but there could be others. During the skill practice, ask Anna for other reasons, even if she volunteers one or two reasons.

Kelley then checks with Mark to see what his objectives are for the discussion:

Think about the critical steps for overcoming resentment and how the manager handled a similar situation in the film, and tell me what you see as your objectives for your discussion with Anna.

Mark:

Well, my overall objectives are to discuss the specific behavior with Anna, to have an open discussion about whether she feels any resentment, and to agree on a specific action that will reduce the resentment if there is any.

Kelley:

Good. You might also remember another overall objective: to correct the dysfunctional job behavior. Anna has curtailed her verbal communications with you, and they need to be reinstated.

Kelley then asks Mark to describe briefly how he will handle specific critical steps. In this particular case, Critical Steps 1, 3, and 6 can be preplanned, so the chances of a successful skill practice are increased. Kelley responds to each question with information about the situation or suggestions for how to handle it. Finally, she checks with Mark to see whether he has any other questions about the skill practice:

Mark:

Suppose Anna continues to deny any resentment toward me during the skill practice?

Kelley:

If that happens, you will not be able to complete Critical Step 3, "Discuss sources of resentment, including yourself." In other words, you cannot discuss the sources of resentment if Anna denies resent-

ment. If that does occur, ask Anna to avoid the behaviors you mentioned in Critical Step 1 and ask for suggestions on how to improve the situation. If she makes suggestions, then begin a problem-solving discussion like the one in "Improving Employee Performance." If she has no suggestions, reiterate your hope that she will correct the situation mentioned in Critical Step 1. Ask her to be responsible for changing her behavior. You should end the discussion at that point.

After dealing with Mark's questions, Kelley asks him to spend a few more minutes preparing for the skill practice while she coaches Anna.

Then Kelley works with Anna to help her prepare for the employee's role in the skill practice. Her approach with Anna is similar to her approach with Mark. She asks for and deals with Anna's initial questions and concerns about doing the skill practice; then she asks several questions to determine how well Anna understands the content of the skill practice:

What do you think your supervisor is going to discuss with you?

What are your feelings toward him?

Do you feel resentment toward him? Why or why not?

Kelley then discusses Anna's objectives for her discussion with Mark. Anna's objectives are to discuss her feelings toward Mark and the reasons for her resentment in an open, nonthreatening manner. If the discussion becomes threatening, Anna will discuss her on-the-job behavior, but not her feelings. Kelley then provides Anna with some additional guidelines about how cooperative or hostile to be, depending on how the discussion with Mark goes. After checking for additional questions or concerns, Kelley completes her coaching.

The entire process of coaching Mark and Anna takes only five or six minutes. Mark and Anna conduct the skill practice, and Mark handles the situation successfully. The rest of the class sees Mark use the critical steps, one by one, in handling the situation and achieving a satisfactory outcome.

After Mark and Anna complete the skill practice, Kelley manages the process of providing Mark with immediate feedback. First, she asks Anna a few questions to establish the value of the discussion from the employee's perspective and to begin the process of feedback to Mark on specific behaviors he used during the skill practice:

As the employee, do you feel your manager listened to you?

Anna:

Yes, I believe he did.

Kelley:

What specifically did Mark do to indicate that he was listening to you during your discussion?

Anna:

When I said I thought he was being unfair when he suspended me, he said he understood my feelings, particularly because he knew other employees had gotten away with the same thing. He said he could see how I could feel his treatment was unfair.

Kelley:

Did you also feel that he was sincere?

Anna:

Yes, especially after he acknowledged my feelings of being treated unfairly. I believed him when he said he was interested in my ideas about possible solutions. He seemed to be really interested in solving the problem, instead of trying to get on my case.

Kelley:

How about it, Mark? Is that what you were intentionally doing?

Mark:

Yes, it was. I wanted to let Anna know I understood her feelings, and I really wanted to reach some agreement on what we could do to resolve the situation.

Kelley:

Did you feel comfortable during the discussion?

Mark:

It was difficult at first. In a real-life situation, I would probably be nervous about telling Anna that she was avoiding talking to me. I felt more at ease as the discussion went on. When we started discussing the reasons, things really went better.

Kelley:

Is there anything you would change about the way you handled the situation?

Mark:

I could have opened the discussion differently, but I'm not sure how.

Kelley:

The observers may have some ideas. Would you be interested in their comments?

Mark:

Yes, anything that would make opening the discussion easier.

Kelley then manages the observers' feedback to Mark. She reminds the observers of the ground rules: State feedback in behavioral terms and address the remarks to Mark—so he can respond if he so wishes. She asks the observers to highlight Mark's accomplishments by providing examples of specific behavior that was effective and to tell him why it was effective. Although the observers are now relatively skillful in the feedback process established in the earlier modules, Kelley must occasionally interject a question or comment to help them frame their feedback with specific and meaningful comments. For example, one observer fails to give concrete details.

Observer:

Mark, you responded effectively when Anna said it was not fair to give her a one-week suspension.

Kelley:

What did Mark say that you thought was effective?

Observer:

He said, "Anna, I know you feel I was unfair in giving you a one-week suspension...but you and I have to work together, and we respect each other's competence. What things can we do to make the way we work together most effective?"

Kelley:

How was that effective?

Observer:

It acknowledged Anna's feelings and moved the conversation forward into a discussion of possible solutions.

Mark indicates that he would also like feedback on how he could have been more effective, so Kelley asks for suggestions. One observer describes what happened in a particular instance and then provides Mark with an APB and gives the rationale for it:

Mark, in Critical Step 1, Anna reacted negatively when you said her second-quarter savings were only half of what they had been in the first quarter. Her response was, "Great! What has the company ever done for me?" You could have avoided that reaction by saying that $125,000 in cost reductions was uncharacteristic of her normal high-level performance and that you wanted to look at the reasons for the decline. This would have put the focus on Anna's usually good performance and suggested that you were interested in removing any barriers to her performance.

Throughout the process, particularly when observers are suggesting APBs, Kelley occasionally checks with Mark to determine whether he is accepting the feedback:

Mark, you said earlier you thought you could have handled Critical Step 1 a little differently. What do you think about that last suggestion?

Mark:

It makes sense. I could have phrased my statement about Anna's cost reductions in less negative terms, and that probably would have avoided the hurdle I mentioned earlier: trouble getting started. Now I think I have a good idea how to take a different tack next time.

After Mark's feedback session, the other learners take turns practicing the managerial skill and receiving feedback. Each succeeding skill-practice situation becomes more difficult. After two more prepared skill practices, Kelley asks each participant to describe a situation he or she is facing on the job. She then works with the participants to write up the situations for the remaining skill practices for this module. Kelley continues to manage the feedback process as she did for the first exercise. This method assures that the feedback will be directed to the skill-practice manager in a way that he or she will accept, so that it will be meaningful and useful in improving skills.

COMMENT

Just as the novice cannot learn to pilot an aircraft by reading a book and watching a film, neither can managers develop managerial skills by those methods. Skill practice and immediate feedback, which are crucial elements of the behavior-modeling process, require management by a competent instructor to make the process truly effective. Successful skill practices and feedback must meet the criteria listed earlier in this chapter, and this can only be accomplished when a competent instructor has diagnosed the needs of the learners and planned the learning experience accordingly. Important competencies required of the behavior-modeling instructor include managing the skill practice and the feedback process for maximum learning in the classroom and easy transfer to the job.

REFERENCE

Knowles, M. Are you an andragog? *IM Navigator,* Spring 1977, pp. 1-2.

8

Management-Reinforcement Skills: Preventing "You Should Have Sent My Boss"

"You should have sent my boss." How often have you heard that statement from supervisors who have attended effective supervisory training but must return to an environment that does not encourage or reinforce their use of these new skills? Obviously, these supervisors have little faith in the support that their managers—or the organization in general—will provide.

FIVE WAYS MANAGERS UNDERMINE SKILL TRANSFER

We will examine five ways that managers can discourage newly learned interactive skills, and then we will discuss how to overcome these obstacles.

1. Lack of Encouragement. Remember Frank Sheppard in the preface to this book? He certainly received no encouragement from his manager to apply his newly learned skills. We could paraphrase his manager and discover what he really meant: "I don't believe in all this stuff they teach. It won't work on the job, so why don't you just do things the way you did before you took that course? I am sure you will be much more effective that way."

When supervisors receive this sort of message, they quickly decide it is much too risky to use the skills learned in the classroom. They ask themselves, "Why should I use skills advocated by the training department when my boss feels they're not worthwhile?" Even if supervisors believe the newly learned skills present a better method for handling on-the-job situations, few will try to use them after being told by their managers that this is not the way to manage people.

2. Lack of Reinforcement. For supervisors to use their newly learned skills over a sustained period of time, the skills must be reinforced. In most cases, lack of reinforcement is not the result of the manager's *disapproval* of the new skills; it simply stems from the manager's lack of awareness about the need to reinforce these skills or lack of the necessary reinforcement skills. Many managers feel that for supervisors to learn the skill in the classroom is sufficient and that actively reinforcing the skill would be a waste of time. However, when no reinforcement is provided, supervisors often assume the manager does not care whether the skills are used.

In many cases, the supervisors' managers do not have the *reinforcing* skills. Although they may want to reinforce, and may even attempt to do so, their lack of skill undermines their efforts. For example, if a manager says, "Well, I see you finally decided to use the skills you learned in that training program; they're supposed to make you a better supervisor," the statement may be perceived by the supervisor as a sarcastic *disapproval*. No matter what the reason, the lack of reinforcement will tend to extinguish the skills the supervisors developed in the classroom.

3. Poor Advice. When supervisors have questions about how to handle specific employee situations, such as introducing change, handling employee grievances, or discussing substandard performance, they often go to their managers for advice. Studies have shown that managers usually provide subordinate supervisors with advice on how to handle such situations. The problem is that sometimes the manager's advice is poor. Managers sometimes advise their supervisors to use methods that are contrary to those learned in the classroom.

When this situation occurs, the supervisor will likely choose the manager's approach, because the penalties for not following the manager's advice are greater than the penalties for not following the advice of the classroom instructor. However, the managers are not purposely giving poor advice; they are simply unaware of the behaviors taught in the classroom.

4. Lack of Coaching. Supervisors often need their managers' help in handling particularly difficult situations. For example, a supervisor may introduce a change that affects several employees. Because the change will have both positive and negative consequences for the employees, the supervisor needs to handle it skillfully. The supervisor is looking for much more than general advice when asking his or her manager how to handle this change. In reality, the supervisor is seeking specific guidance and needs to be coached in particular behaviors that will be most effective. In response, the manager might say something like "You and I support the decision to switch to the new procedure because we know the reasons for the change. I'm confident that the employees in your work group will support the change if they understand the reasons. So let's start by listing all the reasons for the change. Then let's discuss each of the reasons to make sure you are able to explain them adequately to your employees. If you start the conversation this way, I'm sure your work group will be more receptive to the change."

This type of thorough coaching will help the supervisor prepare for the discussion. Unfortunately, many managers do not wish to coach or lack the skill to coach effectively. Therefore, they cloak their advice in concepts and general principles and expect the supervisor to translate them into effective behavior.

For managers to be effective coaches, they need to be able to outline specific behaviors that should be used in given situations.

5. *Different Values*. Sometimes the values of an organization's managers are not compatible with those taught in the classroom. When their managers' values are different, supervisors tend to discard the newly learned skills.

For example, if a group of supervisors has learned the skills of maintaining employees' self-esteem, they will expect their own managers to maintain *their* self-esteem. If the manager fails to do so, not only will the newly learned skills be extinguished, but the supervisors will feel they wasted their time in the classroom. They may also conclude that the managers are inept because they are not using the approach recommended in the classroom.

If the skills being learned by the supervisors conflict with the values of their managers, the supervisors may feel confused or discouraged when they return to the job. The solution to this problem, obviously, is to change either the values of the managers or the content of the workshop—or a combination of the two.

MANAGEMENT-REINFORCEMENT SKILLS

Now that we have established that the problems often stem from managers' lack of skill or from a difference in values (Robinson, 1976), we need to talk about solutions.

You will recall from Chapter 2 the sixth point in the behavior-modeling-decision flow chart: "Will new skills be reinforced?" If your answer was no, the next question was "Can obstacles to reinforcement be overcome?"

An effective way to overcome obstacles to reinforcement stemming from managers' lack of skill is through a management-reinforcement workshop, which would accompany the supervisory-skills-development program. The designer of the management-reinforcement workshop should use the same decision flow chart to determine whether behavior modeling is an appropriate technology for equipping managers with the skills needed to foster supervisory-skill transfer to the job.

The following case example illustrates the general structure and process I recommend for a management-reinforcement workshop.

AN EXAMPLE: THE I.D.A. CORPORATION

Four months ago, Tim Shaffer, the director of training for the I.D.A. Corporation, collected needs-analysis data from the general manager and from the managers and supervisors in the production division. (See Figure 14 for the organization chart.) The data

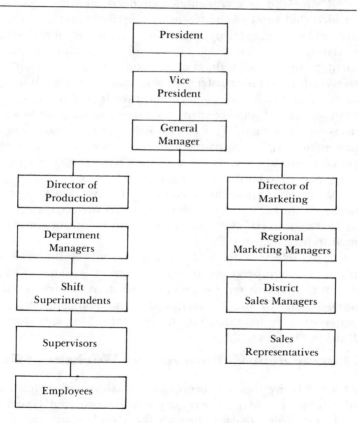

Figure 14. I.D.A. Corporation Organization Chart

indicated that supervisors needed to improve their interactive skills in the areas of discussing employee performance, discussing poor work habits, maintaining improved performance, handling employee complaints, handling employee grievances, resolving grievances effectively, taking effective follow-up action, introducing change, and motivating average performers.

Improved skills in these areas would enable supervisors to conduct more successful discussions with employees, which would—in turn—result in specific, desired changes in employee behavior. In addition, there would be other benefits: Change would be introduced more efficiently, substandard employee performance would be dealt with more effectively, and a greater percentage of grievances would be handled at the supervisory level.

Using the behavior-modeling decision flow chart, Tim decided that most of the learning experience could and should utilize behavior modeling. In considering the question of obstacles to reinforcement, however, Tim found that, within the management group in the production division, several conditions negatively affecting skill transfer existed in some measure. Although no one manager lacked all the skills required for reinforcement, each manager lacked some of them. By using the behavior-modeling-decision flow chart, Tim determined that a management-reinforcement workshop, using behavior modeling as part of the process, would provide the managers with the knowledge and skills needed to reinforce the supervisors' skills.

It became apparent, therefore, that two workshops were needed in the I.D.A. Corporation: one to instruct supervisors in the needed managerial skills and one to train managers in management-reinforcement skills.

After selecting the modeling displays and skill practices and planning the supervisors' training program, Tim designed a 2½-day management-reinforcement workshop, which would be attended by all the production-division managers before the supervisors started their training program. The agenda are outlined in Figure 15.

Management-Reinforcement Workshop: Day 1

Program Objectives. Tim begins the workshop with a presentation of the objectives of the supervisory-training program. He explains that a main objective is to provide the front-line supervisors with the skills they need to handle specific employee situations effectively that were identified through a needs analysis. He summarizes the skills in the titles of the ten modules in the program:

1. Improving Employee Performance
2. Discussing Poor Work Habits
3. Maintaining Improved Performance
4. Taking Effective Follow-Up Action
5. Taking Disciplinary Action
6. Handling Employee Complaints
7. Handling Employee Grievances
8. Resolving Grievances
9. Introducing Change
10. Motivating Average Performers

Tim explains that the program will help supervisors develop necessary interactive skills and that the I.D.A. Corporation should receive the following benefits.

DAY 1 (FULL DAY)

Program Objectives

Program Concepts

Workshop Objectives

Generic Skills

Supervisory-Skill Module 1

Management-Reinforcement
  Techniques

Coaching Supervisors on
  the Use of Skills

Supervisory-Skill Modules
  2 Through 4

DAY 2 (FULL DAY)

Supervisory-Skill Module 5

Reinforcing Supervisors'
  Interactive Skills

Combined Skill Practices:
  Coaching Supervisors on Skill Use
  Supervisory Skill
  Reinforcing Supervisors'
    Interactive Skills

Supervisory-Skill Modules
  6 Through 8

Combined Skill Practices:
  Coaching Supervisors on Skill Use
  Supervisory Skill
  Reinforcing Supervisors'
    Interactive Skills

DAY 3 (HALF DAY)

Supervisory-Skill Modules 9 and 10

Diagnosing Critical Situations

Combined Skill Practices:
  Diagnosing and Coaching
  Supervisory Skill
  Reinforcing Supervisors'
    Interactive Skills

Implementation Issues

Figure 15. Agenda for Management-Reinforcement Workshop

1. There will be fewer instances of substandard performance.
2. The chronically substandard performers will be terminated.
3. A higher percentage of the grievances filed by employees will be resolved in a manner satisfactory to the organization.
4. When changes are introduced, there will be fewer grievances and greater efficiency.

Tim and the managers then discuss the objectives and planned results of the present workshop. Concerns are listed and goals are clarified.

Program Concepts. This section of the workshop highlights the skill-building aspects of the supervisors' training program and demonstrates how managers' behaviors can affect favorably or unfavorably their supervisors' use of skills.

Tim reviews the primary objectives of the supervisors' program: to provide supervisors with sufficient information about various procedures and then to develop the skills needed to implement those procedures. The supervisors would be trained in procedures for handling grievances, dealing with substandard performance, praising above-standard performance, taking disciplinary action, and handling progressive discipline.

Tim then describes the skill-building process and explains how specific skills will be developed. He also outlines the behavior-modeling learning process, emphasizing and describing its key elements: behavioral, instructional objectives (critical steps); positive, credible models; skill practice; and immediate feedback. He then points out that even though the skills are developed in the classroom, the key to the program is the successful transfer of those skills to the job.

Tim also emphasizes that the managers are crucial to this transfer. Using several examples, he points out how managers have already been effective in reinforcing their supervisors' newly learned skills. The corporation's safety program is one of these areas. He also cites a few instances, such as performance appraisals, in which managers have, in effect, discouraged on-the-job application of supervisory skills.

Workshop Objectives. Tim outlines the objective of the management-reinforcement workshop: to provide managers with the skills and knowledge necessary to reinforce supervisors' newly learned skills in order to ensure the supervisors' continued use of the skills over a sustained period of time. He outlines the manager's role as reinforcer, advisor, coach, and positive model, then leads a discussion of what each role requires.

The purpose of this section of the workshop is to acquaint managers with the skill-building and knowledge objectives of the workshop and to clarify their role in providing for transfer and ongoing use of skills by supervisors.

Generic Skills. Tim explains that the supervisors' program also provides opportunities to learn generic skills that can be used in all discussions with employees. The generic skills to be learned in the supervisors' program are the following:

- Maintain or enhance the self-esteem of the other person.
- Listen and respond with empathy.
- Ask for the other person's help and ideas.

These generic skills are thoroughly discussed so each manager knows how and when supervisors will use them.

Supervisory-Skill Module 1. In this part of the workshop, managers participate in the first skill module in the supervisors' program, "Improving Employee Performance." The module is conducted exactly as it would be for supervisors, with one exception: Only two skills practices are offered. Not all of the managers need to participate in this particular skill practice. The reasons for requiring any of them to participate are to acquaint managers with the behaviors that supervisors will use in handling performance-improvement discussions with employees, to demonstrate the behavior-modeling learning experience, and to demonstrate that the critical steps really work.

Management-Reinforcement Techniques. In this part of the workshop, managers examine techniques they can employ to fulfill their roles of reinforcers, advisors, coaches, and positive models. Tim's presentation and the managers' discussion concentrate on the specific techniques that are effective in fulfilling each role:

- As reinforcers, they can recognize and praise supervisors who use the newly learned skills back on the job.
- As advisors, they can help subordinate supervisors diagnose employee problems and advise them on which skills to use in a given situation.
- As coaches, they can provide supervisors with specific behavioral coaching on how to handle employee discussions.

- As positive models, they can reinforce the supervisors' newly learned skills by demonstrating the same skills.

Coaching Supervisors on the Use of Skills. Tim uses behavior modeling to train managers how to coach supervisors. The managers participate in skill practices in which they provide "supervisors" with specific behaviors for handling interactions with employees. Tim uses the same techniques for preparing the participants and managing feedback as he would use in a supervisory-skill module.

Supervisory-Skill Modules 2 Through 4. After a couple of skill practices, the managers spend the rest of the day participating in each of the next three modules of the supervisors' program: "Discussing Poor Work Habits," "Maintaining Improved Performance," and "Taking Effective Follow-Up Action." The managers do one skill practice from each of these modules to become familiar with and to try out the behaviors the supervisors will be using on the job.

Management Reinforcement Workshop: Day 2

Supervisory Skill Module 5. Day 2 begins with the managers' participation in "Taking Disciplinary Action," a fast-moving skill module with one skill practice.

Reinforcing Supervisors' Interactive Skills. This is the first segment of the workshop that deals specifically with the manager's role as reinforcer. This segment uses behavior modeling exclusively, including a modeling display and skill practices on reinforcement. The objective is to develop skills for providing supervisors with recognition when they use a newly learned skill.

The managers first learn the critical steps for reinforcing supervisors' skills:

1. Refer to a specific situation handled by the supervisor.
2. Review the critical steps used in the situation.
3. Discuss any problems the supervisor had in handling the situation.
4. Come to an agreement on how to handle such problems.
5. Compliment the supervisor for using the new skills.
6. Encourage the supervisor to continue using the new skills.

The modeling display portrays a manager as he follows these critical steps in a discussion with a subordinate supervisor. After viewing the display, each manager participates in a skill practice and receives feedback from the others in the classroom.

The steps in reinforcement are designed not only to reinforce supervisors in utilizing skills, but also to uncover any problems they may be having with them and to give advice on how to handle the problems.

Combined Skill Practices. In this section, the managers link the skills of coaching with the skills of reinforcing. The skill practice has three parts and requires three participants. In the first part, a manager coaches a supervisor on how to use a particular skill in a predetermined situation with an employee. In the second part, the supervisor has the discussion with the employee. In the third part, the supervisor and the manager review the discussion, and the manager uses the critical steps for reinforcing a supervisor's skills.

After each part of the skill practice, the observers provide feedback about the things the manager or supervisor handled well and about behaviors that could be improved.

Supervisory-Skill Modules 6 Through 8. This is a fast-moving overview of three supervisory-skill modules: "Handling Employee Complaints," "Handling Employee Grievances," and "Resolving Grievances." Tim outlines the content, the managers watch the modeling display, and one skill practice is conducted.

Combined Skill Practices. This is a second opportunity for the managers to link their coaching and reinforcing skills. This skill practice also contains three parts: The manager coaches the supervisor on how to use the skills, the supervisor has the discussion with the employee, and then the manager and the supervisor talk about that discussion so that the manager has an opportunity to reinforce the supervisor's interactive skills.

This skill practice may center around a prepared exercise, or the managers may elect to develop an exercise from one of their own situations on the job.

Management-Reinforcement Workshop: Day 3 (Half Day)

Supervisory-Skill Modules 9 and 10. The day starts with a quick examination of two supervisory-skill modules, "Introducing Change" and "Motivating Average Performers." In each case, Tim briefly presents the module content and the managers view the modeling display. In each module, one skill practice is conducted.

Diagnosing Critical Situations. This exercise provides managers with skill in diagnosing employee situations. Tim gives the managers descriptions of employee situations that commonly occur within the I.D.A. Corporation. Each manager diagnoses the problems and selects appropriate supervisory-skill modules. The managers' individual selections are analyzed, and a "best answer" is determined for each situation.

Combined Skill Practices. This is the final three-part skill practice. In the first part, the manager helps the supervisor diagnose an employee situation and select the most appropriate critical steps. Then the manager coaches the supervisor on how to handle the critical steps and the discussion with the employee.

In the next part, the supervisor uses the information from the coaching session in a discussion with the employee. In the third part, the manager and supervisor discuss what happened when the supervisor met with the employee. The manager reinforces the supervisor's use of interaction skills and suggests solutions if the supervisor encountered any problems in the employee discussion.

Implementation Issues. During the entire 2½ days, the managers have been compiling a list of concerns. Tim leads a discussion in the last hour of the workshop to help the managers analyze these concerns and discover steps they can take to overcome them.

For example, the I.D.A. managers are concerned about their supervisors' reactions when they see that all managers are following the same critical steps in reinforcing the supervisors' skills and coaching them on the use of the critical steps. Tim addresses this issue by saying that it is acceptable for the supervisors to know that the managers are using skills and critical steps they have learned in the management-reinforcement workshop. A more serious concern should be that managers might *not* be seen using the skills. By using them, the managers demonstrate to the supervisors that they believe in the program. In addition, they indicate that they expect supervisors to use their own newly acquired skills. Tim explains that managers have various personalities, which will produce differences in the ways they implement the critical steps.

At the end of the workshop, Tim re-emphasizes the purpose of the management-reinforcement skills to provide a reinforcing climate for supervisors. The key concept propounds that if managers employ their newly learned reinforcement skills on the job, supervisors will use their own newly learned skills.

Positioning the Management-Reinforcement Workshop

After designing the management-reinforcement workshop, Tim had to determine who should attend. In examining the production division, he realized that all levels of management above supervisor interacted with the supervisors and, thus, needed to develop management-reinforcement skills. This group included the general manager, the director of production, department managers, and shift superintendents (see Figure 14).

Tim did not think that the president and the vice president needed to attend the management-reinforcement workshop, because they did not communicate directly with the target audience, the supervisors. However, they would be involved in a management-support meeting of the type described in Chapter 9.

In examining the shift superintendent's job, Tim and his staff discovered that shift superintendents often interacted with production employees. It became apparent that the shift superintendents needed to learn both the management-reinforcement skills and the interactive skills covered in the supervisors' program. A special mid-level program was developed to provide the shift superintendents with both sets of skills. The mid-level workshop (outlined in Figure 16) is a combination of the supervisors' program and the management-reinforcement workshops.

Day 1	*Day 2*
Introductory Module	Supervisory-Skill Module 3
Supervisory-Skill Module 1	Supervisory-Skill Module 4
Supervisory-Skill Module 2	Supervisory-Skill Module 5

Day 3	*Day 4*
Review of On-the-Job Use of Skills	Review of On-the-Job Use of Skills
Supervisory-Skill Module 5 (continued)	Supervisory-Skill Module 7 (continued)
Supervisory-Skill Module 6	Review Module
Supervisory-Skill Module 7	Supervisory-Skill Module 8

Day 5	*Day 6*
Review of On-the-Job Use of Skills	Reinforcing a Supervisor's Interaction Skills
Supervisory-Skill Module 9	Diagnosing Critical Situations
Supervisory-Skill Module 10	Implementation Issues
Management-Reinforcement Techniques	Workshop Evaluation
	Summary

Figure 16. Agenda for Mid-Level Workshop

The three types of workshops would enable the various levels of management at I.D.A. to learn the necessary skills:

- Supervisors would learn the interactive skills suggested by the needs analysis.
- Shift superintendents would learn interactive and management-reinforcement skills.
- Department managers, the director of production, and the general manager would learn the management-reinforcement skills.

ARE THERE ALTERNATIVES TO MANAGEMENT REINFORCEMENT?

Supervisory-development programs have been conducted for years without management-reinforcement workshops. Very little research indicates to what degree supervisors transferred skills to the job when their managers received management-reinforcement training. In 1974 and 1975, Agway surveyed the interactive skills that were used by supervisors on the job seven months after training. The median increase in use was 15 percentage points. Although the managers received a briefing, they were not trained in management-reinforcement skills. An increase of only 15 percentage points seems to be far less than could have been achieved if the managers had attended a management-reinforcement workshop, because a supervisor's increase in skill development in the classroom is usually much greater than 15 percentage points.

The need for management-reinforcement workshops was the result of behavior-modeling training, which was first applied—and is most often used—to provide supervisors and managers with situational skills, such as dealing with substandard performance, discussing poor work habits or absenteeism, taking disciplinary action, and handling employee complaints. In most cases, middle- and upper-level managers do not need to develop these same skills. Therefore, the traditional top-down approach, such as management by objectives (MBO)—in which all levels of management learn the same skills—is not appropriate for reinforcement in behavior-modeling programs. For this reason, management-reinforcement workshops were first offered by Development Dimensions International in 1975 when it launched its Interaction Management System for first- and second-level supervisors. Now, most well-designed behavior-modeling programs offer management-reinforcement workshops when the skills taught to the target audience are significantly different from those required by the middle- and upper-level managers.

Some organizations use managers as instructors. This arrangement provides managers with another opportunity to reinforce the skills. However, even in these cases, the managers should complete a management-reinforcement workshop so they can maximize their roles as advisors, coaches, reinforcers, and models, both on the job and in the classroom.

Even in programs in which managers are taught the same skills as their subordinate supervisors, there is often a need to develop special management-reinforcement skills. For example, in an MBO program in which both managers and supervisors learn negotiating and reviewing-performance skills, the managers still need to know how to advise, coach, and reinforce their supervisors for a successful implementation.

COMMENT

There is little hard evidence to show that management-reinforcement workshops are essential to achieving the sustained use of the target audience's new skills on the job. However, the Agway study indicates that without management reinforcement, the amount of skill transferred from the classroom to the job is less than satisfactory. Other inquiries into skill transfer have yielded hundreds of examples in which little or no on-the-job use of supervisory skills after training can be traced to one or more of the five ways previously mentioned that managers discourage skill transfer.

Data from the Interaction Management System indicate the stated intentions of some managers who have attended management-reinforcement workshops conducted in conjunction with supervisory-skills training (*IM Navigator*, 1979). In a survey of 771 managers, 91.6 percent indicated their intentions to use their management-reinforcement skills, and 91.4 percent indicated they felt their subordinate supervisors would use their newly learned interactive skills.

There seems to be no alternative to management reinforcement at this time. If supervisors are to receive reinforcement from their managers, the managers must be aware of the importance of their roles in skill transfer and must learn the skills needed to fulfill the roles.

REFERENCES

91.6 percent of supervisors intend to use interaction management skills. *IM Navigator*, Summer 1979, pp. 1-2; 22-23.

Robinson, J.C. Don't blame managers—They don't know how. *Training Management & Motivation*, Fall 1976, pp. 6; 30-33; 35.

9

Obtaining Management Support

Even though a management-reinforcement workshop can provide appropriate reinforcement skills, the managers must *want* to reinforce their supervisors' new skills. Because the managers control how and when they reinforce the skill transfer, it is imperative for all managers at all levels to be motivated to support the use of the target audience's new skills.

Research has shown that learners' performance often sags immediately after training, then returns to its pretraining level after a period of time.[9] In the case of supervisory-skills training, the problem frequently extends to the entire work group. Supervisors who develop new skills in the classroom try them on the job. Work-group performance declines briefly as the employees adjust to their supervisors' new behaviors. When supervisors see this drop in performance and receive little or no management support, they gradually abandon the new skills and return to their former methods of managing. When this occurs, employees conclude that everything is back to "normal," and their performance returns to its pretraining level.

What *should* happen after training is depicted in Figure 17. Although performance still drops after supervisors start using the new skills, management encourages the supervisors to continue to use them. These skills make the supervisors more effective, and, thus, employee performance gradually improves.

HOW MANAGEMENT PROVIDES SUPPORT

The type of support needed from management will vary from level to level. In most organizations, support for a management-development program comes from the top managers in several ways:

They Provide the Required Resources. They provide the money to purchase materials and conduct workshops, and they allow the time

---

[9]See, for example, Rackham (1979). Although Rackham eloquently describes this phenomenon in his article, he recommends only coaching by managers as a solution. I believe that the solution consists of all the management-reinforcement and support functions described in Chapters 8 and 9.

needed by supervisors and managers to attend. They also select credible line and staff managers for instructors and provide the resources to train them to be competent instructors.

They Actively Endorse the Skills. They endorse the skills by indicating to managers and supervisors that their use will make supervisors more effective. They also state that the end results will benefit the organization in many ways, e.g., improved morale, increased productivity, and better communication.

They Encourage Use of the Skills. At every opportunity, they urge managers to use the reinforcement skills and supervisors to use the interactive skills. In other words, whenever a situation requires interactive skills or management reinforcement, the top managers advocate them.

They Establish Positive Organizational Reinforcement. The top managers examine sources of reinforcement to supervisors in the organization. They attempt to remove any barriers to using the newly learned skills, they strengthen the present reinforcement, and they provide additional reinforcement. Support sought from middle managers typically takes three forms:

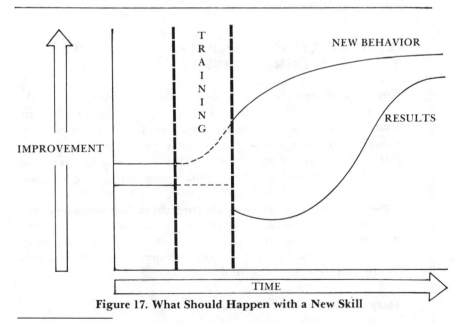

Figure 17. What Should Happen with a New Skill

From Neil Rackham, The Coaching Controversy. *Training & Development Journal*, 1979, *33*(11), p. 14. Copyright © 1979, *Training & Development Journal*, American Society for Training & Development. Reprinted with permission. All rights reserved.

Participating in the Management-Reinforcement Workshop. This participation includes taking time from managers' primary responsibilities to attend the management-reinforcement workshop, to actively participate in the workshop and develop the skills of advising, coaching, and reinforcing, and to be positive models.

Providing Time for Their Subordinate Supervisors To Attend the Supervisory-Skills Program. Attendance requires the supervisors to be away from their jobs during the classroom sessions.

Using the Management-Reinforcement Skills. The skills of diagnosing critical situations, coaching supervisors, reinforcing supervisors' interactive skills, and being a positive model must be used on the job. In addition to learning the skills, the managers must perceive the benefits of the skills and desire to use them on the job.

One of the main concerns before implementing a supervisory-development program is to ensure these primary forms of support from top and middle management. How to obtain management's assurances of its support, of course, varies from organization to organization, depending on the organizational structure, objectives, norms, and values. The following case example illustrates one successful approach for obtaining management's support.

A CONTINUING EXAMPLE: THE I.D.A. CORPORATION

The top-management team at I.D.A. consisted of the president, the vice president, and the general manager (see Figure 14). Tim Shaffer wanted the top-management team to provide support to I.D.A.'s supervisory-skills development program in four ways: (1) to commit the resources required for the training, (2) to endorse the skills to be developed through the program, (3) to encourage on-the-job use of the skills, and (4) to establish positive organizational reinforcers. Support sought from the middle managers—the director of production, the department managers, and the shift superintendents—included participation in the management-reinforcement workshop and a commitment to use the management-reinforcement skills on the job.

Key Manager's Support

Tim's first step was to identify the key manager, i.e., the manager whose support was vital to effective implementation of the supervisory-training program.

The key manager in the I.D.A. Corporation was the general manager. Once the general manager decided that the training program was beneficial, Tim knew he would recommend it to the vice president. Chances were good that the vice president would accept the general manager's recommendation.

With the support of both the general manager and the vice president, Tim assumed the president would endorse it. The president would need only an overview of what the program would do, its costs, and the knowledge that the vice president and the general manager had endorsed it.

If the general manager and the other top managers endorsed the program, Tim theorized that it would be relatively easy to gain the support of the middle managers, but it would not come automatically. Although they might *voice* support for the program, they would have to see real benefits before *actively* endorsing it.

Tim's first step in obtaining the general manager's support was to tell him of his plans for an *in-depth* needs analysis, which would give him information about the type of training needed for I.D.A. supervisors. In earlier conversations, Tim and the general manager had discussed the general need for supervisory training that was uncovered in a *preliminary* needs assessment, and the general manager had outlined what the supervisors needed to be doing more effectively. They had also decided that, in the short run, Tim should concentrate on the production department.

Tim explained that he would send questionnaires to the supervisors and the shift superintendents and individually interview the department managers, the director of production, and the general manager. After tabulating the data, Tim would present the general manager with a recommendation for training the supervisors. He estimated that data collection and analysis would take six weeks. He requested two things of the general manager at this time: (1) his endorsement of the data collection and (2) a meeting with him at the end of the analysis.

The general manager agreed to endorse the data collection and said he would meet with Tim in six weeks. He also requested that other members of his staff be present at that meeting: the controller and the directors of production, marketing, human resources, and transportation.

Tim agreed and indicated his desire to interview these staff members during the data-collection phase. He hoped to obtain their insights into the kinds of problems encountered by the production supervisors. He also wanted to brief them on the purpose of the meeting with the general manager.

The general manager agreed to Tim's proposals, and the first step of the management-support process was completed. The next step was to collect data and prepare for the management-support meeting.

Preparation for the Management-Support Meeting

Tim needed to collect specific data to enable him to deal with the concerns of the general manager and his staff. Before beginning his in-depth needs analysis, Tim had a good idea of the issues that would concern the general manager. Because the general manager had raised the question of what supervisory training was needed, Tim knew he was concerned about the supervisors' effectiveness. Tim was also aware of the general manager's method of management. He was basically a "bottom-line" manager; that is, he collected and analyzed sound operating data to find ways to improve the bottom line.

As Tim collected data, he decided to work on two basic concerns: to determine deficiencies that had a direct effect on the bottom line but could be changed through improved supervisory skills and to determine the type and frequency of discussions that supervisors were having with their employees. In addition, he wanted to determine the level of skill that supervisors possessed for handling each type of discussion.

Data About Supervisors' Skills

Tim wanted to know two things about supervisors and their use of interactive skills: (1) what types of frequently encountered situations required supervisors to use interactive skills and (2) how skillful they were in handling these situations.

Because there were 144 supervisors in the production department, Tim could not interview each one. Therefore, he used a survey instrument (see Figure 18) that consisted of seventy-five items. It covered twenty-five skill areas that were selected on the basis of the initial needs analysis and a review of the literature. They represented specific situations with which supervisors would need to deal.

One hypothesis on which the questionnaire was based was that the higher the frequency of an interaction, the greater the need for supervisors to develop skills in that area. For example, if employee complaints occurred frequently, there would be a strong need for training in handling complaints. The initial needs analysis had simply indicated that supervisors were not interacting

In the columns on the left, indicate the approximate number of times you encountered that situation in the last year. Place a check (   ) in one of the columns.

In the columns on the right, indicate the degree of difficulty experienced in handling that specific situation. Place a check (   ) in one of the columns.

25 or More Times	19 to 24 Times	13 to 18 Times	6 to 12 Times	0 to 5 Times	As a supervisor, you did:	Extremely Difficult	Very Difficult	Difficult	Slightly Difficult	Not Difficult
					1. Take immediate corrective action to correct an unsafe procedure...					
					2. Recognize (at a time other than the employee's performance appraisal or salary review) "above average" output of work being accomplished by an "average" performer					
					3. Discuss a performance (quality and/or quantity of work output) problem with an employee.....					
					4. Talk with an employee who thought he/she was being treated unfairly and who threatened to file a grievance					
					5. Determine an individual employee's performance goals/standards					
					6. Terminate an employee because of poor performance..........					
					7. Discuss an unsafe procedure with an employee					
					8. Explain to an employee how his/her pay level was determined					
					9. Handle an employee complaint.					
					10. Demonstrate step-by-step a job the employee needed to learn ...					
					11. Talk with an employee who was consistently late to work.......					
					12. Handle a discrimination complaint brought to your attention by an employee.............					

Figure 18. Needs-Analysis Form (Partial Contents)

with employees as effectively as they wanted to. Therefore, the most urgently needed training would be in skills to handle the interactions that occurred most frequently.

Tim's questionnaire also asked supervisors to rank types of interactions according to their degree of difficulty. The hypothesis was that supervisors would rate as most difficult those interactions for which they needed the most training. Granted, the perceived difficulty could be either the result of a truly difficult discussion or the lack of an interactive skill. Nevertheless, when a specific interaction was perceived as difficult, the conclusion would be that the supervisor wanted training in that area.

Data from Managers

Tim collected data from thirty-one managers (including the general manager's staff). He identified two types of situations with which supervisors needed to deal: (1) performance deficiencies that affected the bottom line and that could be improved with better use of supervisory and managerial skills and (2) situations in which supervisors handled discussions with employees so ineffectively that managers became concerned. Tim therefore developed a patterned interview that focused on these two items. Figure 19 shows the types of questions that focus on performance deficiencies, and Figure 20 shows a typical series of questions dealing with ineffective supervisory skills.

Data Analysis

When the supervisors' questionnaires were returned and tabulated, the data indicated how frequently the supervisors used each of the twenty-five skills and the relative difficulty they experienced in applying each of them.

In tabulating the information from the thirty-one patterned interviews, Tim was able to isolate twelve major bottom-line areas of concern. He gathered operating data on each and quantified their dollar impact on the bottom line. As soon as Tim organized this information, he was ready to conduct the management-support meeting for the general manager and his staff.

The Management-Support Meeting

In conducting the management-support meeting for the general manager and his staff, Tim used the following agenda:

1. Outline of Meeting Objectives and Agenda
2. Outline of Performance Data

3. Outline of Supervisory-Skills Data
4. Proposed Training Approach: Behavior Modeling
5. Possible Program Designs
6. Management Reinforcement
7. Required Resources
8. Decision: To Go or Not To Go

1. Outline of Meeting Objectives and Agenda. Tim first outlined the objectives and the agenda of the meeting. He told the managers the meeting had been called to examine and discuss the

---

What three operating areas in your department do you see as having the greatest potential for improvement?

Area of Improvement _____

Unit of Measurement _____

Current Performance _____

Realistic Potential Performance _____

Impact in Dollars (from Current Performance to Realistic Potential Performance)

Comments:

How can supervisors (in your department) affect this area of performance?

How can employees (in your department) affect this area of performance?

**Figure 19. Patterned Interview for Managers: Cost-Benefit Analysis
(Partial Contents)**

Try to recall a situation that had a negative impact on the I.D.A. Corporation or on an employee that could have been prevented if it had been handled properly by a supervisor.

1. What was the general type of situation?

2. What was the negative impact?

3. What led up to the situation?

4. Relate the events that occurred when the supervisor interacted directly with the employee(s).

5. How many discussions did the supervisor have with the employee?

6. Describe other discussions (concerning this same subject) that the supervisor had with the employee. Were they handled appropriately or inappropriately?

7. Describe in detail one of those discussions.

8. How was the overall situation resolved?

9. Who was the key person in resolving the situation? Specifically, what did this person do to resolve the situation?

10. What were the key factors in resolving this situation?

Figure 20. Patterned Interview for Managers: Critical Incidents (Partial Contents)

needs-analysis data. Tim said he would provide enough data throughout the meeting for the managers to decide whether the proposed supervisory training would be cost beneficial and whether it was important enough to be implemented in the production division. Although the meeting was structured to allow Tim to present the data and a recommendation, he encouraged an informative discussion to help the managers make a decision by the end of the meeting.

2. Outline of Performance Data. Tim outlined the performance data obtained through the patterned interviews. The data related to the four major departments in production: doors and doorframes, windows and window frames, wood panels, and molding. (In the interest of conserving space and time, the remainder of this case example will refer to the performance data pertaining only to the wood panels department. The same process for discussing data would be utilized for the other three departments.)

Tim detailed four major performance criteria for the wood panels department, as cited in the interviews with the management group. These included quantity (number of panels produced per day), quality (error rate, based on the number of rejected panels), housekeeping, and preventable accidents. Because the quantity goal was being achieved, managers indicated that they wanted to see improvement in quality, housekeeping, and preventable accidents.

Tim said the 2 percent error rate meant that 1,440 panels were being rejected each day—exactly twice the standard error rate. These panels were sold at a $2 discount, thus costing the organization $1,440 per day more than standard.

There appeared to be no way to quantify savings for improved housekeeping. Although most of the managers had indicated that better housekeeping would improve the company's image and morale, they were unable to put a dollar value on it. Many managers felt that improved housekeeping would reduce the accident rate—the third item to be measured. The managers found preventable accidents were costing the wood panels department $144,000 per year in lost time and additional insurance premiums. Therefore, performance deficiencies in the wood panels department were costing the company $489,600 per year (see Figure 21).

3. Outline of Supervisory-Skills Data. Tim then reported that all managers had said that supervisors could improve their interactive skills. He also related some general examples of situations that had negative effects on profitability. He cited a specific situation in which an employee had misunderstood a supervisor's directions, resulting in the rejection of several hundred panels. In another situation, an employee had presented a complaint to a supervisor and, because of the supervisor's mishandling of that complaint, the employee filed a grievance.

Tim then summarized the needs-analysis data, focusing on the frequency and relative difficulty of the twenty-five skills (Table 5). The data showed how many times per year supervisors had specific discussions with employees and how difficult they felt each type of discussion was. For example, the average supervisor had twenty-seven discussions per year with employees about work habits. These discussions were perceived by supervisors as "difficult." Supervisors introduced change into their work groups about six times a year and found these discussions "very difficult." Tim explained that this information would help determine which skills should be included in the supervisory-training program.

4. Proposed Training Approach: Behavior Modeling. Next, Tim discussed behavior modeling: how it builds both skill and confidence in supervisors and how it deals with specific supervisory situations. He stressed that the purpose of behavior modeling is to develop skill and confidence to such a level that the supervisors would use their new skills on the job.

Population		Production	
	1 Department Manager	Production of Panels	
	7 Shift Superintendents	3-Shift Operation	
	48 Supervisors		
	300 Employees		

I. CRITERIA

		Goal	Actual
Quantity	Panels per Day	72,000	72,000
Quality	Error Rate	1%	2%
Housekeeping		All Areas Clean Housekeeping Orderly	Partially Clean Partially Orderly
Preventable Accidents		None	24 per Year

II. AREAS OF DEFICIENCIES

Criteria		Cost of Deficiency
Quality	720 Panels per Day @ $2.00 $1,440 per Day for 240 Days	$345,600
Housekeeping		No Measurable Savings
Preventable Accidents		144,000
Total		$489,600

III. TARGETED IMPROVEMENT

		Value of Correcting Deficiency
Quality	Reduce Error Rate by .5%	$172,800
Housekeeping	All Areas Clean Warehousing Orderly	No Measurable Savings
Preventable Accidents	Reduce by 33 1/3%	48,000
Total Value		$220,800

IV. COST OF IMPLEMENTING SUPERVISORY TRAINING

	Costs
Training Supervisors: 48 @ $360 (Salaries)	$ 17,280
Training Shift Superintendents: 7 @ $220 (Salaries)	1,540
Training One Manager: (Salary)	250
Training One Instructor: (Salary and Travel)	975
Purchase of Software	9,583
Total Costs	$ 29,628

V. COST-BENEFIT RATIO

$$\frac{\text{Value of Correcting Deficiencies}}{\text{Cost of Implementing Training System}} = \text{Return on Investment}$$

$$\frac{\$220,800}{\$ 26,278} + 8.4 + \text{Return on Investment}$$

Table 4. Cost-Benefit Analysis for Supervisory-Skills Training

Tim then walked the group through a skill module. He covered the skill-module introduction, discussed the critical steps, and showed and discused the modeling display. He then conducted one skill-practice feedback session. Then he ended the skill module, and the manager discussed what had taken place.

5. *Possible Program Designs.* In introducing the discussion of possible program designs, Tim reviewed the areas of deficiency highlighted in the needs-analysis summary. The group made suggestions about how the deficiencies could be reduced, provided that supervisors received the proper training in the appropriate skills. Supervisors' use of the following skills, for example, would reduce the quality deficiency:

- *Improving Employee Performance.* When an employee is having problems with performance quality, the supervisor and the employee can discuss how to overcome them and reach agreement on activities that will improve performance.

- *Improving Work Habits.* When the supervisor recognizes a poor work habit, the supervisor and the employee can discuss how to overcome it.

- *Taking Effective Follow-up Action.* When initial discussions do correct the problems, the supervisor can conduct follow-up discussions to indicate that improvement is still necessary and to reach agreement on new activities to overcome the problems.

- *Recognizing Improved Performance.* When an employee's performance has noticeably improved, the supervisor can give positive reinforcement by recognizing the improvement.

- *Teaching Employees on the Job.* When employees do not have the skills to produce quality work, the supervisor can teach them those skills.

- *Motivating the Average Performer.* When employees are unmotivated, the supervisor can encourage them in several ways to improve performance. For example, the supervisor can recognize their abilities or the tasks they do well.

In the discussion that followed, Tim and the managers outlined programs that would help supervisors develop skills to reduce performance deficiencies.

6. *Management Reinforcement.* Next, Tim briefed the general manager and his staff on the need for management reinforcement. He outlined the critical roles of the manager as reinforcer, advisor,

Table 5. Summary of Needs-Analysis Data

Organization_____ Unit_____Date_____

Department _____

I.D.A. Corporation   Production   2/9   Wood Panels

SKILL MODULE	SUPERVISOR N = 41		MANAGER N = 7	
	Frequency	Difficulty	Frequency	Difficulty
1. Orienting the New Employee	5.54	1.25	10.81	1.03
2. Improving Employee Performance	23.06	1.58	16.11	1.92
3. Improving Work Habits	27.00	1.34	22.78	1.75
4. Improving Attendance	6.73	1.57	18.33	1.72
5. Reducing Tardiness	3.46	1.26	6.22	1.72
6. Maintaining Improved Performance	19.69	1.41	9.06	1.61
7. Utilizing Effective Follow-Up Action a. General: Employee Performance and Work Habits a.	2.93	2.28	8.00	2.63
b. Specific: Telephone, Attendance, Safety, Housekeeping b.	3.39	1.40	7.80	2.04
8. Utilizing Effective Disciplinary Action a. Warning a.	5.50	1.62	5.78	2.00
b. Suspension, termination, formal b.	1.93	1.87	3.38	2.52
9. Handling Employee Complaints	25.29	1.81	42.64	2.09

10. Overcoming Resistance to Change	6.21	1.60	6.11	1.94
11. Delegating Responsibility	25.23	1.24	30.11	1.67
12. Setting Perfor-mance Goals	4.67	1.40	6.56	1.91
13. Reviewing Perfor-mance Goals	3.48	1.48	7.03	1.87
14. Motivating the Average Performer	33.69	1.26	18.89	1.78
15. Teaching an Employee a New Job				
a. By Supervisor a.	8.73	1.60	15.39	1.71
b. By Key Employee(s) b.	21.96	1.29	13.33	1.56
16. Handling Customer (Client) Complaints				
a. Handled By Supervisor a.	1.48	2.00	0.11	3.00
b. Handled By Employee(s) b.	0.00	0.00	0.00	0.00
17. Handling Emotional Situations	3.31	2.69	3.67	3.13
18. Handling Discrim-ination Complaints	2.00	2.32	2.78	2.69
19. Taking Immediate Corrective Action	29.36	1.60	13.88	2.12
20. Gaining Accept-ance as a New Supervisor	2.20	2.77	3.28	2.79

OTHER AREAS

Setting Performance Goals (Upward)	3.11	1.37	2.00	1.88
Reviewing Performance Goals (Upward)	18.21	1.20	4.00	1.43
Dealing with Union or Union Steward	19.13	1.50	32.00	1.69
Discussing Serious Work Rule Violation (Upward)	3.82	1.27	17.75	1.29
Dealing with Employee Dishonesty	0.30	2.00	0.75	2.14

coach, and positive model. He explained how a manager can affect supervisors positively or negatively and mentioned that the manager is a major factor in determining whether or not the supervisor uses the skills on the job.

7. Required Resources. Tim outlined the resources required from the general manager and his staff. These included cash expenditures ($26,278 for the wood panels department) and the salaries of the supervisors, shift superintendents, and managers who would attend the workshops.

In addition to financial resources, the general manager and the staff would also be asked to look at organizational reinforcement. To clarify this concept, Tim cited an I.D.A. policy that discouraged supervisors from handling employee complaints: a requirement that all complaints from employees be written on a special form before any action by management. Because of the tedious writing job, many supervisors did nothing about complaints. This policy would present a significant obstacle to skill transfer.

Another important resource, Tim told the managers, was their active endorsement of the skills. Supervisors would need to realize that managers really wanted them to use the skills, and management's endorsement would be vital to the success of the training program. One purpose of the management-support meeting, Tim said, was to provide managers with sufficient information to make a decision about whether to endorse the supervisory skills.

8. Decision: To Go or Not To Go. The decision "to go or not to go" centers around two questions: Is the program cost beneficial and does the program have a high priority?

In examining the cost-benefit ratio, Tim said the managers in the wood panels department believed that a reduction of .5 percent in the error rate—a savings of $172,800—within the first year was reasonable. There would be no measurable savings for improved housekeeping. Managers also felt that preventable accidents could be reduced by one-third for a saving of $48,000.

Thus, the value of correcting the deficiencies was $220,800, whereas the cost of the training would be only $29,628. This would provide a return on investment of 7.45. In other words, the department would receive a 745 percent return on the amount of money invested in the training program.

As is often the case, one of the managers asked about reducing the length of training to three days and, therefore, increasing the return on investment. When they examined the modules that would have to be cut out to shorten the program, the group determined the objectives they had set could not be achieved with fewer modules.

The group also agreed the training was a high priority item. Therefore, the general manager's staff recommended that the program be implemented as soon as possible and completed within a year. The general manager concurred. The management-support meeting ended with a commitment by the general manager and his staff to the whole package: training in interactive skills for supervisors and a management-reinforcement workshop for managers.

Top-Management Support

Now that the general manager had decided to implement the training, he needed the approval of his immediate supervisor, the vice president. He arranged for a meeting in which he and Tim would repeat Tim's management-support presentation. Because only those three people would attend and because the vice president's time was limited, the general manager and Tim estimated that they could cover all the material in an hour.

The vice president also approved the plan, leaving the president as the last member of top management to be approached for support. It was customary for the I.D.A. president to concur when the general manager recommended a program and the vice president approved it. Therefore, the general manager briefed the president on the proposed training and the president concurred with his recommendation.

Middle-Management Support

Now that top-management support for the program was lined up, support would be needed from the middle managers. Even though top management had committed the financial resources, middle-management support was required in the form of actively endorsing the skills, developing management-reinforcement skills, and examining organizational reinforcers. This support was imperative, because the middle managers would be expected to reinforce supervisors directly and, therefore, they would need to learn the skills of reinforcing, advising, coaching, and being a positive model. In addition, they would need to use those skills on the job. Even though middle managers could be required to attend the management-reinforcement workshop, they could not be forced to encourage supervisors to use the skills on the job. Tim knew it was essential to have a management-support meeting for each level of middle management.

Following the agenda for the first management-support meeting, Tim met with the director of production and his four department managers. The general manager was present to indicate that he had recommended the training and to assure the department managers that each should base the decision for his own department on the cost-benefit ratio. The department managers were also asked to make independent decisions on whether the training was important enough to implement within the next year.

Managers of the wood panels department and the door and door frames department wanted to implement the program immediately. The others decided to postpone it for at least six months.

Tim then conducted management-support meetings with the shift superintendents in the two departments that were taking immediate action. The department managers and Tim followed the same overall agenda except, they presented only data that pertained to the particular department.

The meetings with the shift superintendents differed from the previous meeting in one important respect: the department managers stated that the decision to conduct the program had already been made and asked the shift superintendents to help make the training successful by using the interactive skills, by using the management-reinforcement skills, and by actively endorsing the program and the skills. Therefore, the meetings were introductions to changes.

Tim also requested a thirty-minute meeting with the shift superintendents in the departments that postponed the training. He gave them an overview of the training for the other departments and explained why they had decided to implement the training immediately. He and their department managers also explained why the training had been postponed in their departments.

When Tim finished this series of meetings, the management-support phase was complete. Tim and his staff could now gear up to conduct the management-reinforcement workshops and the supervisory-skills training. The entire management-support process, including data gathering, took fifteen weeks. However, the process produced a crucial net result: Tim had obtained top-management support and full support from the departments that were implementing the training. In addition, the other department managers knew they could decide not to implement the training without being penalized.

OTHER APPROACHES

This type of management-support meeting is only one approach to management support. However, it is representative of the most effective approaches, particularly when needs and potential outcomes can be quantified and communicated to management in bottom-line terms.

Needs and outcome data cannot always be quantified—much less translated to dollar cost-benefit ratios—so different approaches to conducting presentations to gain management support are also appropriate. At Agway, for example, when Paul Steiger and I were asked to examine the needs of the supervisors, we did not attempt to quantify the data or the benefits of training. Instead, the objectives for training the physical distribution division were presented simply as follows:

1. To phase in the new physical distribution centers as scheduled.
2. To develop and maintain a supportive work climate as perceived by the employees.
3. To induce supervisors to work directly with the employees, rather than through a third party.

Agway management felt that accomplishing these three objectives far outweighed the cost of the training program.

At General Electric in Evendale, Ohio, behavior-modeling training by Mel Sorcher in the early Seventies was designed to reduce the turnover of new employees. The number of new employees retained after training was a 150 percent improvement, and this outcome was sufficient for management to support the program, even though it was not directly translated to bottom-line savings.

A variety of other objectives would be appropriate to examine in a management-support meeting—such as reducing the number of grievances, improving customer relations, or improving interdepartmental relations. Management-support meetings can also deal with objectives related to preventing problems or maximizing opportunities.

SUMMARY

Management support is crucial to the success of any behavior-modeling program. Granted, the training director may be pressured to train before obtaining management support, and this pressure may come from management itself. However, if true management support does not exist, the training should be postponed. This is particularly important for training that uses behavior modeling, because supervisors will not use the skills on the job unless they receive reinforcement and because managers will not reinforce unless they *want* to. They must understand and be committed to the need for the supervisory training, the role of management reinforcement, and the benefits to them and the organization. An effective approach to accomplishing this is the management-support meeting. Once support meetings have been conducted at all levels in the organization, the training can take place. An investment of fifteen weeks by Tim Shaffer and his staff assured management support and greatly increased the probability that managers and supervisors would use their newly learned skills on the job.

REFERENCE

Rackham, N. The coaching controversy. *Training and Development Journal*, 1979, *33*(11), 12-16.

10

Evaluation:
What Management
Wants and Needs To Know

We usually think about evaluating a program to give the training department an idea of how effective the training has been. However, another important objective of an evaluation is to help line management determine whether a particular training program should be continued, expanded, or discontinued. The recommended approach to this type of evaluation is based on three actualities in the operation of organizations:

1. Line management makes the final decision about management development in the organization. Although the training department conducts the programs and workshops for managers, it cannot perform without line management's support and approval. If the management-development function is going well, line management will support it with resources; but if a training program is not meeting the needs of line management, it will probably be changed or discontinued.

2. Line management judges the effectiveness of all management training, whether or not planned evaluation is taking place. If one goes into any organization and asks the line managers how effective their management-development program is, the line managers—in almost every case—will have made judgments about its effectiveness and impact on the organization. These judgments are based on whatever data are available, regardless of how limited or unreliable the information may be.

3. Line management controls the resources for management development. In virtually all organizations, the final decision about allocation of resources is made by line management. The line produces the product or provides the service and makes the profit. The line also allocates resources to those areas that will contribute most to providing products and services and producing a profit. The management-development effort is only one of

many functions seen by line management as an aid to achieving its mission. If line management judges that the management-development effort is making a significant contribution, it will support the effort with resources: the money for the training staff and materials and the time for managers and managerial candidates to participate.

In the future, resources will be even more scarce than they are today. Therefore, management will have increasingly greater problems allocating resources to all functions within the organization, including training. Because of declining resources, management will insist that all functions become more accountable. Therefore, all organizational units, including training, will need to provide management with more substantive and reliable data about their contributions. A training department would have to find out what management needs to know and wants to know about the training function in the organization, and it would need to establish a method for providing management with substantive, reliable data in a useful format.

THE OVERRIDING QUESTION

Management's overriding question about a management-development program is "Should it be continued, expanded, or discontinued?" To make that decision, line management needs specific information:

1. Are the needs that were identified in the needs analysis being met by the training program?
2. To what degree are the skills learned in the training program being used on the job?
3. What return on investment is the organization receiving from the training program?

Line managers often ask a fourth question: What are the reactions of those who have been trained in the management-development program? Although the training community may see reaction measurement as a superficial or unimportant evaluation, this sort of data can have as much impact on managers' decisions to continue, expand, or discontinue a program as does any other. Many good programs have been eliminated because of negative reactions by participants. Additionally, a disproportionate amount of negative information about training programs is fed back informally to line managers, because a few participants who have negative feelings about the experience are often more vocal than are those who react favorably. Therefore, management needs a summary of reactions by *all* participants.

One challenge that a training manager faces in evaluating a program centers around the fact that many organizational line managers have not been educated in what to ask about the effectiveness of the management-development effort. Therefore, the training manager should involve them in the evaluation process.

HOW TO DESIGN AN EVALUATION STUDY

There are eight major steps in designing an evaluation study that will involve line managers and answer their questions.

1. Define the purpose of the evaluation study. Give line management the information it needs to determine whether to continue, expand, or discontinue the behavior-modeling program for managers.

2. Identify the decision makers. Identify the specific line managers who will be making decisions about the program. Many times an executive committee, a budget committee, or a human-resources committee includes some or all of the key decision makers.

3. Specify the needed information. In general, the decision makers need information that answers the questions that were previously listed in this chapter under the heading "The Overriding Question." Knowing what questions to ask, of course, is only one part of this step. The specific type of information that the key decision makers *want* must also be determined, and the information that is submitted to them must be credible.

4. Determine where the information can be obtained. After the *type* of information is established, the source of such information must be determined. These data may already be tabulated somewhere in the organization. They key to this step is not only to find the data, but also to determine whether or not they can be used in their present form.

5. Determine the overall design of the evaluation study. An experimental design that can be easily understood by the line managers should provide them with reliable data. The key is to offer alternative evaluation designs and to test them out with the line managers.

6. Determine how to gather the data. Data-gathering methods that are the least costly and burdensome to the organization should be used. When line managers hear the term "evaluation," they often think that considerable time and money will be involved. For data that are not already available in an acceptable form, establish a collection method that is efficient and simple.

7. Determine how to analyze the data. The process for analyzing the data must be developed before the data collecting begins. Too often, people collect data only to find out that they cannot make a meaningful analysis. Thorough planning will avoid that error.

8. Determine how to feed the data back to management. This is best handled by asking managers for their preferences. Do they prefer to have a written report or an oral presentation? Would they like the data fed back quarterly or monthly? The key here is to find out how to assemble the data in a format that management will be able to use to make the necessary decisions.

The overriding objectives for developing an evaluation study are to focus on what management wants and needs to know and to keep it simple.

There are many ways to approach evaluation. Ten different people will ofer ten different recommendations on how to design an evaluation study. I recommend the approach outlined on the preceding pages for the evaluation of behavior-modeling management-development programs because:

- It is directed toward the decision maker, the line manager.
- It involves the line manager.
- It is a simple, pragmatic approach to evaluation.

There are a couple of disadvantages to this approach: First, it is intended for internal use. Therefore, if the need to publish an evaluation study exists, this approach will probably not meet that need. Also, this approach is subject to criticism by the professional and the academically trained evaluator. Often there will not be a control group or statistical analysis. Therefore, the evaluation would be vulnerable to criticism by those who advocate a more formal, statistically rigorous approach.

All evaluation projects require resources, mainly time and money. These resources will be drawn from the primary mission of the training function: the development of skills and knowledge. Therefore, an inherent concern in all evaluation studies is obtaining the necessary resources. It is imperative, therefore, that the evaluation be valuable enough to outweigh the costs of designing and implementing it.

AN EXAMPLE: THE NATURAL NUTRITION NUTS COMPANY

The Natural Nutrition Nuts Company (3-N), a chain of three hundred retail stores throughout the United States, features a complete line of health foods. The chain has recently been growing at a rapid rate, adding about thirty stores per year. Because of its growth, the average length of service for store managers is four years with the company with two years as store managers.

Most 3-N store managers are high-school graduates who started as clerks in the retail stores. After demonstrating good job performance and an interest in retailing, they were promoted to assistant managers in larger stores. After working as assistant managers for about a year, they were given their own stores. Their training as assistant managers consisted of learning as much as possible about store operations from their store managers.

Most stores have about ten employees: the store manager, three full-time employees, and six or seven part-time employees. The 3-N Company runs a lean operation, which provides good profits from high volume. The territory is divided into three regions of about one hundred stores each. Each regional director supervises six or seven district managers, each of whom has about fifteen stores in his or her district.

The health food business is very competitive. To attract customers, the stores must be clean and efficient. Due to the limited experience of the store managers, particularly in supervising, some necessary job duties were not being satisfactorily performed. The two areas of concern were less-than-satisfactory housekeeping and merchandising. The stores looked messy, merchandise was neither attractively displayed nor convenient for the customers to reach, and sales were declining.

In a regional staff meeting, the regional director (Dick Cadwell) discussed the housekeeping and merchandising problem with his merchandising manager (George Joworski) and his human-resources manager (Barbara Carter). Dick wanted to correct the problem and asked for their help. George agreed that the poor in-store merchandising was negatively affecting sales. Although George had been working with the store managers, he had been unable to make satisfactory progress. He said the store managers claimed that because they had to rely so heavily on part-time help, they were not able to fulfill some of the job requirements. Barbara Carter said that she would like to collect more data from the store managers and employees before making a specific recommendation on how to deal with the problem. Dick agreed with her approach.

Barbara then conducted one-on-one interviews with the store managers and a sampling of the employees. She found that most of the store managers were concerned about the poor housekeeping and in-store merchandising. They were frustrated by the situation, because they felt that, regardless of how hard they worked, their employees did not cooperate. They said they had to push their employees all the time to get anything done. Barbara's needs analysis also surfaced the fact that many of the employees felt that the supervisors were giving them "a hard time" rather than working with them.

After Barbara analyzed the data, she concluded that the managers would be more effective if they could improve their interpersonal skills in dealing with employees. The complete data revealed that the poor housekeeping and merchandising were only two of several problems. A professional shopping service had conducted a survey a year earlier that indicated that customers did not think the store employees were courteous. Employees said in their interviews with Barbara that they felt their managers did not listen to them and sometimes treated them unfairly. She also found a significant amount of confusion about work rules and procedures among the employees.

Barbara discussed her findings with Dick and George. She recommended that the store managers in their region be trained via a behavior-modeling program that would improve their interpersonal skills for dealing with their employees. She also recommended that the seven district managers in the region be provided with management-reinforcement training. She further suggested that the training be handled in three phases.

Phase 1 would deal with the problems of poor housekeeping and poor in-store merchandising. The store managers would be provided with the skills needed to assign tasks clearly to employees, to work with employees on improving their performance, and to help the employees feel that their managers were working with them.

Phase 2 would provide the store managers with the skills needed to handle the growing number of complaints from employees and customers. Phase 2 would be implemented six months after the completion of Phase 1.

Phase 3 would be implemented fifteen months after the completion of Phase 1. It would teach managers the skills needed to feed back to employees the results of a customer survey, which was scheduled for a year after the completion of Phase 1. The managers would also be able to work with employees to develop recommendations for improving store operations and the work environment.

The training would not only help the organization improve

its performance, but it should improve customer relations and revenue. In addition, it should change the work environment from confrontive to collaborative.

Dick was willing to start Phase 1 but would not implement Phases 2 and 3 until he was sure that Phase 1 had been effective. Barbara told Dick that an evaluation would provide him with the information he needed to determine whether the program should be continued or discontinued after Phase 1.

After receiving Dick's commitment to proceed and to support the program, Barbara began to work with him and George to plan and implement the evaluation. She used the eight steps previously discussed in this chapter.

1. Define the purpose of the evaluation study. The team members (Dick, George, and Barbara) agreed that the purpose of the study in their region was to provide management with sufficient information to make a decision on whether or not to proceed with Phase 2 after Phase 1 was completed.

2. Identify the decision makers. They also agreed that Dick was responsible for the decision to implement Phase 2. Although he would ask for inputs and recommendations from Barbara and George, the final decision was his.

3. Specify the needed information. Dick would need information to answer the following questions:

- Did Phase 1 improve in-store merchandising?
- Did Phase 1 improve housekeeping?
- After Phase 1, did the employees feel that their supervisors were giving them sufficient direction on what needed to be done in these areas and sufficient recognition when it was done? Did they feel that supervisors were working with, rather than against, them?
- Were the skills learned in Phase 1 being utilized by the managers on the job?
- Did the managers have a positive reaction to Phase 1?

Initially, Dick said that he wanted to try to measure increases in store revenues that would result from Phase 1. The assumption was that neat, attractive stores with well-merchandised items would attract more customers and increase revenue. In examining this question more thoroughly, however, the team decided that so many factors contributed to changes in revenue and that to isolate the effects of improved merchandising and housekeeping would be very time consuming and costly. Therefore, they decided that tracking impacts on revenue would not be worth the investment.

4. Determine where the information can be obtained. The team then outlined the sources of information needed to fulfill the purpose of the evaluation (see Figure 21).

In brief, the effect on merchandising would be measured by directly observing the merchandising practices in each retail store, including promoting the "Feature of the Week," displaying posters and banners, having shelves fully stocked, and having all items priced.

The stores were also identified as the sources of data to measure the effect on housekeeping. Direct observation would yield measurements in four areas of housekeeping: neat and clean showroom, neat and clean displays, clean and attractive store front and entrance, and well-organized and clean storage area.

To measure changes in employees' perceptions of their store managers, data would be collected directly from the employees about their understanding of their managers' directions, their feelings of being recognized by the managers, and their perceptions that their managers were working with them, not against them.

The store managers would be the sources of data about their own use of the skills on the job and their reactions to the training.

5. Determine the overall design of the evaluation study. The team decided to take measurements on the items listed in Figure 21 before and after training if possible. These pre- and post-training measurements could then be compared to determine the effectiveness of Phase 1. Pre- and post-training measurements were feasible for the effect on merchandising, housekeeping, and employee perceptions of their managers, but only post-training data could be collected for the managers' reactions to the program.

Dick wanted to implement the training in all the stores in his region, so it was not feasible to set up a control group. He discussed with the other two people the feasibility of using stores in another region as controls, but they decided the time required to organize such an effort and collect the data would not be worthwhile.

6. Determine how to gather the data. The key to this step was to gather maximum reliable data at a minimum expense. Therefore, the team designed a data-collection process that was simple and straightforward. To address each problem area, the team established the following collection methods:

Information Needed or Wanted	Source	Method of Data Collection	Data Collection	
			Frequency	Timing
A. Impact on Merchandising				
(1) Promotion of the "Feature of the Week"	Retail Store	Direct Observation	Weekly	Pre- & Post-Training
(2) Display of posters and banners	Retail Store	Direct Observation	Weekly	Pre- & Post-Training
(3) Fully stocked shelves	Retail Store	Direct Observation	Weekly	Pre- & Post-Training
(4) Fully priced merchandise	Retail Store	Direct Observation	Weekly	Pre- & Post-Training
B. Impact on Housekeeping				
(1) Neat and clean showroom	Retail Store	Direct Observation	Weekly	Pre- & Post-Training
(2) Neat and clean displays	Retail Store	Direct Observation	Weekly	Pre- & Post-Training
(3) Clean and attractive store front and entrance	Retail Store	Direct Observation	Weekly	Pre- & Post-Training
C. Employees' Perceptions of Store Managers				
(1) Employees' understanding of their managers' directions	Employees	Questionnaire	One month before training; three and nine months after training	
(2) Employees' feelings of being recognized by their managers	Employees	Questionnaire	One month before training; three and nine months after training	
(3) Employees' feelings that their managers are working with them, not against them	Employees	Questionnaire	One month before training; three and nine months after training	
D. Store Managers' Skills Used on Job	Store Managers	Do Not Measure	Not Applicable	Not Applicable
E. Store Managers' Reactions to Training	Store Managers	Questionnaire		End of Phase 1
F. Increased Store Revenue	Store Revenue[a]	Do Not Measure	Not Applicable	Not Applicable

[a]Changes in store revenue would be a function of many other variables.

Figure 21. Regional Plan for Evaluation Data Collection

- *Impact on Merchandising.* The data would be collected by the seven district managers, Dick Cadwell, and George Joworski. Weekly store inspections would allow them to fill out a sheet designed to evaluate the four merchandising practices previously discussed. One copy of the sheet would be left with the store manager; a second copy would be sent to Barbara.

- *Impact on Housekeeping.* They would use the same approach for gathering data about housekeeping. Both sets of data would be collected during the same inspection.

- *Employee Perceptions of Clear Directions, Appropriate Recognition, and Cooperation from the Store Manager.* This data would be collected by a questionnaire given to one hundred full-time and one hundred part-time employees. One full-time and one part-time employee would be randomly selected from each store. The data would be solicited from the employees within one month before the beginning of Phase 1, then twice more—three and nine months after the completion of Phase 1.

- *Skill Usage by Managers.* The team wanted data about on-the-job use of the skills by the managers. The members debated feasible approaches for data collection and concluded that direct observation was the only reliable method. Because of the amount of time required, however, they decided not to measure the managers' on-the-job use of the skills. Dick suggested that an improvement in in-store merchandising and housekeeping and a perception by employees that their managers were providing clear directions, giving sufficient recognition, and working in a more collaborative manner would indicate that the store managers were using the skills on the job.

- *Positive Reaction to the Training.* Each store manager would fill out a questionnaire at the end of Phase 1.

7. Determine how to analyze the data. All data would be sent to Barbara Carter, who would enlist the aid of the corporate data-processing unit. After tabulating the data, Barbara would analyze them to draw tentative conclusions.

8. Determine how to feed the data back to management. Within four months after the completion of Phase 1, Barbara would meet with Dick and George to review the data and her tentative conclusions. Dick would then decide whether to implement Phase 2. This timetable allowed them four months to collect data on the impact of the innovations to in-store merchandising and housekeeping. It also ensured that they would have the three-month post-test information about the employees' perceptions of their managers.

COMMENT

A well-planned and well-executed accountability evaluation will provide management with the data it needs to make informed decisions. This type of evaluation, however, requires advance planning, as well as knowledge about and skill in evaluation design and data-collection and data-analysis techniques. Granted, many training professionals do not have the technical knowledge and skills to carry out evaluation studies, but the requisite expertise can be obtained via contracts with internal specialists or external consultants. Most large organizations employ specialists in several of the following fields: human resources, organization development, research and development, industrial psychology, information systems, data processing, and market research. These, of course, are just a few of the available internal resources. When the training staff wants to evaluate its efforts, internal people are generally very cooperative.

An evaluation to help management make informed decisions can be conducted at moderate cost and without a complex experimental design. The data collection and analysis can be straightforward and uncomplicated. Even though evaluation requires an investment of time and money, the benefits far outweigh the costs.

What the Research Says About Behavior Modeling

A review of available research was made to discover what it says about behavior modeling. Nearly twenty studies detail the effectiveness of behavior modeling. Although most are published, some remain unpublished. Although a few are superficial, most of them are quite detailed. Nevertheless, from each study we can learn something. Each has unique data about the effectiveness and limitations of behavior modeling. Several of the studies use the same experimental design with different audiences. Some of the characteristics and uses of behavior modeling have been evaluated several times. Other characteristics and uses have not been evaluated at all.

If we could display all the data from the evaluation studies on one large surface, we would have an unfinished picture. In certain areas, the data are clear and distinct; in other areas, no data are available; in still others, we have only partial data. This unfinished picture, however, gives an overview and helps in visualizing what behavior modeling can and cannot do.

The research becomes more clear when the studies are grouped into the four evaluation categories defined by Kirkpatrick (1976):

1. Reaction Measures. These report the participants' reactions to the learning experience.

2. Learning Measures. These indicate the amount of learning that took place during the learning experience.

3. Behavior Measures. These reflect the amount of learning that is actually applied on the job.

4. Results Measures. These are measurements of the impact that learning has had on the organization in terms of performance change.

REACTION MEASURES

We will examine four of the published reaction-measurement studies on behavior modeling. These four studies range from the reactions of some twenty supervisors to a survey of 8,255 supervisors. Latham and Saari (1979) reported on the reactions of twenty supervisors in the Weyerhaeuser Company in Aberdeen, Washington. This study measured the extent to which supervisors felt that behavior-modeling training helped them do a better job of interacting more effectively with employees, peers, and superiors. In each of four ratings, the supervisors' reactions were favorable immediately after training, and eight months after training the supervisors reacted even more favorably in the four measures. These results indicate that eight months after training, the supervisors still felt that they were using the skills effectively on the job and that the skills remained helpful to them.

In the American Telephone & Telegraph (AT&T) study (1975), 91 percent of forty-four supervisors reported that three months after the training, they felt that the training had been useful. In Dupont's Sabin River Works (Waltz, 1981) 97 percent of 160 supervisors trained in behavior modeling felt that the newly learned skills were highly applicable to their jobs.

Probably the most extensive reaction-measures study in behavior modeling was conducted by DDI (Development Dimensions International, 1981), which involved supervisors and managers throughout the United States and Canada who had been trained in its interaction management program. At the time this book went to press, DDI had surveyed 8,255 supervisors and 1,820 of their managers, all of whom had participated in a DDI Interaction Management Program conducted by their own instructors in their own organizations. At the end of their training, supervisors were then asked to complete evaluation questionnaires to give their reactions to the program. The questionnaires were given to the classroom instructor, but the supervisors provided the same data on cards that were mailed directly to DDI. The same procedure was used for managers who participated in management-reinforcement workshops conducted by the organizations' staff trainers.

The supervisors rated the program in four areas: the likelihood of using the skills, the applicability of the skills, general satisfaction with the workshop, and satisfaction with workshop procedures. The results in Table 6 show the percentage of supervisors responding favorably or very favorably in each of these areas. Approximately 93 percent of the supervisors felt that they would probably use the skills on the job, and some 91 percent felt that the skills were applicable and indicated satisfaction with the workshop and the procedures used.

The 1,820 managers were asked to report on the likelihood that their subordinate supervisors would use the skills, as well as the applicability of the skills for those supervisors. They were also asked to report on their own likelihood of using the management-reinforcement skills and on their own satisfaction with procedures used in the workshop. These results, shown in Table 7, indicate that more than 90 percent of the managers felt that their supervisors would use the skills, that the skills were applicable for the supervisors, and that they intended to use management-reinforcement skills. Perhaps the most impressive figure is that 95 percent of the managers reacted favorably or very favorably when asked if they would use the management-reinforcement skills.

We may wonder what the reaction measures tell us. In the studies mentioned, a high percentage (usually more than 90 percent) of the trained supervisors said the behavior-modeling skills were useful and applicable to their jobs. Also, more than 90 percent of their managers said they would use management-reinforcement skills and predicted that the supervisors would use the interactive skills. Therefore, we may conclude that well-designed, well-implemented behavior-modeling training for supervisors and managers produces a high percentage of

---

Table 6. Supervisors' Evaluation of the Interaction Management Program

Supervisors' Perceptions of:	Response of "Favorable" or "Very Favorable"
Likelihood of Using Skills	93.5%
Applicability of Skills	91.8%
General Satisfaction with Workshop	91.7%
Satisfaction with Workshop Procedures	91.0%
N = 8,255	

Table 7. Managers' Evaluation of the Interation Management Program

Managers' Perception of:	Response of "Favorable" or "Very Favorable"
Likelihood of Supervisors' Using Skills	93.5%
Applicability of Skills for Supervisors	94.1%
Likelihood of Using Management-Reinforcement Skills	95.2%
Satisfaction with Workshop Procedures	88.9%
N = 1,820	

Source of Data for Tables 6 and 7: *Interaction Management Program Evaluation Norms.* Pittsburgh: Development Dimensions International, 1981.

participants who see the skills as useful and applicable and who plan to use the skills on the job.

LEARNING MEASURES

American Telephone & Telegraph (1974), Central Telephone Company (1975), Lukens Steel Company (King & Arlinghaus, 1976), Medical Group Management Association (DeHaan, Thornton, & Waldman, 1979), Norden Laboratories (Judt, 1978), Weyerhaeuser Company (Latham & Saari, 1979), and Orange County HSA/Social Services (Carillo, 1979) have conducted studies to measure the amount of learning in behavior-modeling training programs for supervisors and managers. Most of these studies use a similar experimental design, incorporating simulations as a method of evaluating supervisors' skills.

Rather than attempting to look at all the studies, we will take one close look at the AT&T study. Completed in 1974, this study was one of the first in behavior modeling that specifically attempted to measure the amount of learning that took place in the classroom.

Ninety supervisors in the trained group and ninety-three in the control group participated. The two groups were matched to reflect similar backgrounds in terms of gender, age, department, experience, and number of subordinates. The supervisors were randomly chosen for the experimental and the control groups.

Members of the trained group participated in a behavior-modeling program involving situations such as discussing quality and quantity of work, dealing with absenteeism, and providing feedback. The control group received no training. Approximately two months after the training, all supervisors, trained and untrained, participated in three simulated problem discussions. Each supervisor held the discussion with a specially trained individual, who played the role of the supervisor's subordinate. The subordinate was unaware of the purpose of the study, but was asked to respond consistently to each supervisor in accordance with the supervisor behavior.

Each supervisor handled three problems: excessive absenteeism, a complaint of discrimination, and a suspected theft. In each case, the supervisor was given background information and time to prepare and then was asked to handle the discussion with the subordinate effectively.

Each discussion was observed by four assessors, who had been trained in behavior observation and in the use of a rating scale constructed specifically for the evaluation. Different assessors were used in each trial, and none was informed about the nature of the trial or the experimental conditions.

The results of the evaluation are shown Table 8. The assessed skill levels of the control group were distributed almost equally among "exceptionally good or above average," "average," and "below average or poor." In the trained group, however, 84 percent of the supervisors were rated "exceptionally good or above average," whereas only 6 percent were rated "below average or poor."

The studies at Central Telephone, Lukens Steel, Norden Labs, and Weyerhaeuser used essentially the same approach as the AT&T study, and the results were generally the same.

Therefore, an important generalization based on these evaluations of learned skills would be that behavior modeling can be an effective method for developing interactive skills in supervisors and managers.

BEHAVIORAL MEASURES

Studies dealing with on-the-job application of the newly learned skills have been conducted by Agway (Byham, Adams, & Kiggins, 1976), AT&T (1974), Rhodesian National Railways (Petasis, 1977), Medical Group Management Association (DeHaan, Thornton, & Waldman, 1979), Norden Laboratories (Judt, 1978), Weyerhaeuser Company (Latham & Saari, 1979), Orange County HSA/Social Services (Carillo, 1979), and the University of Chicago Hospitals and Clinics (Nicholson, 1979). The studies used various approaches, all of which were aimed at

---

Table 8. Percent Distribution of Overall Ratings Made by AT&T Evaluation Panel

Assessed Skill Level	Trained	Control
Exceptionally Good or Above Average	84%	33%
Average	10%	34%
Below Average or Poor	6%	33%
	100%	100%

Number of Trained Supervisors = 90
Number of Control Supervisors = 93

Source of data: AT&T, Management Selection and Development Research, Human Resources Development Department. *Supervisory Relationships Training: A New Approach to Supervisory Training* (Results of evaluation research). New York: Author, 1974.

gathering information about how effectively supervisors handled discussions with employees before and after training. Some employed self-reported data from the supervisors; in others, the evaluators interviewed the supervisors. In still another approach, people who worked with the supervisors (e.g., their managers, peers, or employees) rated the supervisors.

Again, it is impossible within the scope of this chapter to examine all these studies in depth. The Weyerhaeuser evaluation (Latham & Saari, 1979) provides a good example of application measures, and some significant conclusions can be drawn from it. Forty supervisors were randomly assigned to a training or control group. Twenty supervisors were in each group. Their managers were asked to rate them on thirty-five items on behavioral observation scales, which were developed as a result of a job analysis of effective and ineffective supervisory behavior. Managers responded on a five-point scale to rate the extent to which they observed the supervisor demonstrating the behavior. The ratings were conducted one month before and one year after the training. Because the managers knew who were in the training group, they received intensive instruction on how to minimize rating errors.

In the premeasures, there was no significant difference between the trainees and the control group; however, the postmeasure indicated that the trained group performed significantly better (see Table 9).

The managers also rated the supervisors' performance on the company's standard performance-appraisal instrument, which used a five-point scale for twelve behavioral items. The managers did not know

Table 9. Weyerhaeuser Superintendents' Overall Ratings of Supervisors' Job Performance

Instrument	1 Month Before Training		1 Year After Training	
	Trainees	Controls	Trainees	Controls
Behavioral Observation Scale	No Significant Difference		3.47	2.98
Performance Appraisal	No Significant Difference		3.80	3.30

Five-point rating scale
Number of Trained Supervisors = 20
Number of Control Supervisors = 20

Source of data: G.P. Latham and L.M. Saari, Application of Social Learning Theory to Training Managers through Behavior Modeling. *Journal of Applied Psychology*, 64, no. 3 (1979): 239-246.

the ratings were being used to evaluate the effectiveness of the training progam. Neither did they know that the researchers had access to the appraisal forms. Again, there was no significant difference between the trainees and control supervisors on the premeasure, but there was a significant difference on the postmeasure.

The combined results from the analyses of the observation and performance appraisal indicated that supervisors trained with behavior modeling performed more effectively on the job than did the control group.

A similar study was conducted by the Medical Group Management Association with supervisors in the health field to measure the effects of behavior-modeling training. The administrators of the 110 supervisors rated them in eighteen areas of supervision before training and eight months after training (see Table 10). The average rating after training

Table 10. Administrators' Mean Ratings of Supervisory Ability in Eighteen Areas for 1977 Group

Area of Supervision	Pre-Training	Post-Training (8 Months Later)
Administering Discipline	6.36	8.43
Following up Lack of Improvement	7.45	9.30
Dealing with Performance Problems	8.04	9.84
Reducing Tardiness	8.15	9.65
Dealing with Poor Work Habits	7.60	9.55
Handling Employee Complaints	8.55	10.00
Setting Goals	6.37	8.86
Handling Emotional Situations	7.98	9.96
Overcoming Resistance to Change	8.58	10.29
Dealing with Physicians	7.28	9.63
Motivating the Average Performer	7.57	9.55
Discussing Problems Between Departments	8.44	9.86
Handling Client Complaints	8.59	10.11
Solving Problems in a Work Group	7.61	9.30
Motivating the Long-Term Employee	8.20	9.80
Teaching an Employee a New Job	8.91	10.62
Maintaining Improved Performance	8.05	9.90
Delegating Responsibility	8.49	10.09
AVERAGE RATING	7.90	9.71

Number of Administrators = 49

was 9.71 on a ten-point scale, versus 7.90 before training. In every category, the administrators rated the supervisors as more effective after training.

Other studies employing on-the-job application measures have produced similar results. Therefore, we may conclude that when behavior-modeling training is effectively conducted and when supervisors are encouraged on the job to improve and change, the supervisors will use their newly learned skills and, as a result, will become more effective.

RESULTS MEASURES

Evaluations that measure results are most complex and difficult. Therefore, we would expect fewer studies and have been able, in fact, to locate only five significant studies in this area.

One study was conducted at the University of Chicago Hospitals and Clinics (Nicholson, 1979). Twenty-six supervisors rated changes in seven areas of their work groups. The results are shown in Table 11. More than 75 percent of the supervisors felt that their employees had improved in the quality of production and in attitude and morale. About half the

Table 11. Supervisors' Ratings of Changes Within Their Work Group (Chicago Hospitals and Clinics)

| | Supervisors' Ratings | | | |
Areas Rated	Better	No Change	Worse	Don't Know
Quality of Employee Production	20	5	0	1
Employee Attitude and Morale	20	4	0	2
Quantity of Employee Production	11	12	0	3
Employee Promptness	14	10	0	2
Employee Attendance	13	10	1	2
Employee Turnover	1	16	2	7
Employee Complaints and Grievances	10	12	0	4

Number of Supervisors = 26

Source of data: J. Nicholson. *Interaction Management Supervisory Training Evaluation Study*. Unpublished study, University of Chicago Hospitals and Clinics, 1979.

supervisors perceived an improvement in quantity of production, promptness, attendance, and complaints and grievances. In only one area, employee turnover, did the majority of supervisors feel that there was no change. In only three instances was a "worse" rating given.

A study involving forty-four supervisors was conducted at AT&T (1975) to determine the relationship between classroom performance and the change in measured job results. More than half the supervisors showed improved job results three months after training (see Table 12). Supervisors in the lower third of the class showed the greatest improvement in measured job results, and supervisors in the top third showed the least improvement. This trend is understandable, because the supervisors in the lower third of the class probably started with the poorest interactive skills and, therefore, probably had the most difficulty on the job. During the class, they did not surpass the other supervisors, but they improved significantly. Therefore, improvement in their skills would result in improvement in job results. Conversely, managers in the top third of the class were probably more effective supervisors with less room for improvement.

At IBM, managers in branch offices were trained to feed back opinion-survey information to their employees and to prepare meaningful action plans to improve morale (Smith, 1976). Eighteen branch managers were trained, and a control group of thirteen branch managers was drawn from offices matched by geographic location, size, and level

---

Table 12. AT&T Supervisors' Overall Performance in Class and Change in Measured Job Results

Overall Performance During Training*	Measured Job Results**		
	Worse	Same	Better
High [a]	0%	53%	47%
Average [b]	0%	36%	64%
Low [c]	0%	20%	80%

*As rated by course instructors.
**As reported by supervisors three months after training.

[a]Number of Supervisors = 15
[b]Number of Supervisors = 14
[c]Number of Supervisors = 15

Reprinted by permission from *Analysis and Evaluation of Supervisory Relationships Training* (Internal report). New York: American Telephone & Telegraph, 1975, p. 31. Copyright © 1975 by American Telephone & Telegraph.

of employee satisfaction. The behavior-modeling training covered the skills of presenting survey data to employees, accepting their ideas, soliciting their feelings, asking for employee interpretations, and taking notes. The managers were also asked to submit action plans to their immediate managers.

Four months after training, a forty-seven-item effectiveness questionnaire was given to the employees of managers in both the trained and control groups. Employees of trained managers rated the feedback as more effective: 31 percent, versus 20 percent for the control group. Employees of trained managers also rated the meetings as providing more open discussion on relevant issues and generating good ideas from problem solutions.

An opinion survey was also conducted one year after training. As shown in Table 13, the employees of the trained managers changed their opinions dramatically in a positive direction. The overall company-morale index for both groups had been the same before training. After training, the trained group showed a significant positive change in the ratings of the company, earnings, the amount of work, the manager, advancement, and overall satisfaction.

Perhaps it is appropriate that the last studies we will examine are those done at the General Electric Company, because GE was the

---

Table 13. IBM Opinion-Survey Results:
Differences Between Trained and Control (% Favorable)

	Trained Minus Control Before Training	Trained Minus Control After Training
Company	−2%	+11%*
Commitment to Company	−1	+3
Earnings vs. Other Companies	+2	+9
Job Satisfaction	−3	0
Amount of Work	+4	=13*
Ratings of Manager	−1	=10*
Ratings of Advancement	−1	=8*
Overall Satisfaction	−7	=10*

*(p < .01)

Reprinted by permission from P.E. Smith. Management Modeling Training to Improve Morale and Customer Satisfaction. *Personnel Psychology*, 1976, *29*(3), p. 354. Copyright © 1976 by *Personnel Psychology*.

company with which Mel Sorcher began his work in behavior modeling with first-line supervisors. Because of Sorcher's positive results at GE, other organizations, such as AT&T, IBM, and Agway, moved ahead as pioneers in this "new" field. The GE studies are regarded as a turning point in defining the effectiveness of behavior modeling.

In the study at the GE jet-engine plant in Evendale, Ohio, supervisors and their employees were trained via behavior modeling to interact more effectively with one another (Burnaska, 1976). The employees were newly hired minorities with minimal work experience. The behavior-modeling training was initiated because very few of the newly hired minorities had remained on the job for more than six months. Table 14 indicates the results of the study. The retention rate for the trained group was more than 2½ times that of the control group.

In another GE study (Goldstein & Sorcher, 1974), four first-line supervisors were trained via behavior modeling. Their work groups were compared to other work groups with untrained supervisors. A performance measure provided an index that reflected the effective utilization of employee and equipment resources as calculated by the following formula:

$$\text{Performance} = \frac{\text{Actual Productivity}}{\text{Standard Productivity}}$$

Actual productivity was measured as a production level achieved by employees within a production cycle. Standard productivity referred to the production level that management estimated the employees should achieve during a given production period. The performance of the eight work groups was measured ten weeks before and ten weeks after training. The net change in performance in each work group is shown

---

Table 14. Retention of Newly Hired GE Employees After Six Months

Group	Employees Still Working
Trained	72%
Control	28%

Number of Trained Employees = 39
Number of Control Employees = 25

Source of data: R.F. Burnaska. The Effects of Behavior Modeling Training upon Managers' Behaviors and Employees' Perceptions. *Personnel Psychology,* 1976, *29*(3), 329-335.

in Table 15. Data analysis indicated the performance efficiency was significantly higher for workers reporting to supervisors who had participated in behavior-modeling training.

Two issues are relevant to the interpretation of the GE performance data. The first concerns practical significance. A small percentage of increase in productivity was of great practical significance, because a 1 percent overall increase in this case represented a savings of many thousands of dollars per year. The second issue is the large drop in productivity by all the control groups. The general business conditions were very bad during the term of the study and apparently resulted in perceptions of poor work climate and actual drops in productivity. However, the comparatively better productivity indicates that the supervisors who participated in the behavior-modeling program were able to manage the effects of the uncertainty accompanying the poor business climate.

In examining these five studies dealing with organizational performance change, again we ask what the research tells us. The answer is that when behavior-modeling training is selected to meet a specific, organizational performance need and when that training is well implemented, it can have significant impact on the organization.

Table 15. Net Change in Performance (in Percentages) for GE Groups Supervised by Trained and Untrained Foremen

Group[a]	Trained Net Change	Group[b]	Untrained Net Change
T_1	=6%	U_1	-20%
T_2	=4%	U_2	-7%
T_3	=0.1%	U_3	-21%
T_4	-9%	U_4	-21%

$$\text{Performance} = \frac{\text{Actual Productivity}}{\text{Standard Productivity}}$$

[a]Number of Foremen = 4
[b]Number of Employees = 100 (approximately)

Reprinted by permission from A.P. Goldstein and M.A. Sorcher. *Changing Supervisor Behavior.* Elmsford, NY: Pergamon Press, 1974, p. 79. Copyright © 1974 by Pergamon Press.

CONCLUSIONS

We have examined in depth about a dozen studies concerned with behavior modeling. Although the picture is not complete, it is clear enough to draw some conclusions:

- Supervisors and managers react favorably to well-designed behavior-modeling programs and see a usefulness in the application of the learned skills.

- Supervisors and managers can significantly increase their skills through training via behavior modeling.

- Supervisors and managers will use those newly learned skills on the job if they are provided with a supportive climate.

- Behavior-modeling programs can have a significant impact on an organization if the organization uses the training to help solve performance problems.

REFERENCES

American Telephone & Telegraph, Human Resources Development Department. *Analysis and evaluation of supervisory relationships training* (Internal report). New York: Author, 1975.

American Telephone & Telegraph, Management Selection and Development Research, Human Resources Development Department. *Supervisory relationships training: A new approach to supervisory training: Results of evaluation research.* New York: Author, 1974.

Byham, W.C., Adams, D., & Kiggins, A. Transfer of modeling training to the job. *Personnel Psychology,* 1976, *29*(3), 345-349.

Carillo, F. *A report on the evaluation of the interaction management program* (Internal report). Santa Ana, CA: Orange County HSA/Social Services Staff Development Division, 1979.

Central Telephone Company. Unpublished study. Lincoln, NE: Author, 1975.

DeHaan, T.J., Thornton, G.C., III, & Waldman, D.A. Supervisory training produces positive changes in self-confidence and job performance. *Medical Group Management,* March/April 1979, pp. 28-32.

Development Dimensions International. *Behavior modeling evaluation studies* (Unpublished collection, rev.). Pittsburgh, PA: Author, 1981.

Goldstein, A.P., & Sorcher, M.A. *Changing supervisor behavior.* Elmsford, NY: Pergamon Press, 1974.

Judt, J.P. *An evaluation of first-line supervisor skill training.* Unpublished master's thesis, University of Nebraska, 1978.

King, H.D., & Arlinghaus, C.G. Interaction management validated in the steel industry. *Assessment and Development,* 1976, *3*(2), 1-2.

Kirkpatrick, D.L. Evaluation of training. In R.L. Craig (Ed.), *Training and development handbook* (2nd ed.). New York: McGraw-Hill, 1976.

Latham, G.P., & Saari, L.M. Application of social learning theory to training supervisors through behavior modeling. *Journal of Applied Psychology*, 1979, *64*(3), 239-246.

Nicholson, J. *Interaction management supervisory training evaluation study.* Unpublished study, University of Chicago Hospitals and Clinics, 1979.

Petasis, A. Behaviour modelling: It can be an efficient training tool. *People & Profits*, 1977, *4*(11), 6-11. A summary of the study appears in *IM Navigator*, Winter 1977, pp. 10-12.

Smith, P.E. Management modeling training to improve morale and customer satisfaction. *Personnel Psychology*, 1976, *29*(3), 351-359.

Waltz, D. What IM has done—and is doing. *IM Navigator*, Winter 1981, p. 17.

Behavior Modeling: The Coming Years

People often ask me, "What changes will be made in behavior modeling in the coming years?" As risky as it may be to make predictions, I will, in this chapter, forecast the future of behavior modeling. If my predictions are accurate, people will believe I am perceptive and foresighted. If my forecast misses the mark, I have some ten years to think up excuses.

WHAT CAN GO WRONG?

Whenever we look at a growing, promising technology, it is advantageous to think about what can go wrong and inhibit its growth. Having had a part in starting several businesses in the last twenty-five years, I have found that in order to ensure business growth, it is wise to examine the areas of vulnerability. Similarly, I feel that part of my responsibility in the field of training and development is to highlight the areas of vulnerability in the behavior-modeling methodology.

Inappropriate Use

Behavior modeling can be used inappropriately. Because the use of behavior modeling is growing rapidly, it runs the danger of becoming a fad (Robinson, 1980). If it does become a fad, it is likely to be applied to training needs when other methods would be more appropriate. There are really two issues here: using behavior modeling when *training* is not an appropriate solution and using behavior modeling when it is not the most *effective* training technology.

To compound this problem, behavior modeling appeals to the learners. Therefore, even when it is used inappropriately, the learners can enjoy the classroom experience. They can have numerous opportunities to try out skills, receive feedback, and really enjoy the experience. The net result is that no one may realize that behavior modeling was used inappropriately and that the skills learned will have minimal positive impact on the organization.

The vulnerability here lies in a tendency to use a methodology because people *like* it, not because it is the most *effective* methodology. For example, many of us have seen video equipment overused in workshops. I attended a three-day workshop in which video equipment was used by the instructor. About six hours of role play and simulations were videotaped. In attempting to use the tapes for feedback, the instructor had difficulty finding the examples that he wanted us to see. However, since most of us took excellent notes—because of our background in behavior modeling—we were able to provide almost verbatim feedback to the role players. The instructor had succumbed to the temptation to use a methodology because it was faddish, whereas a simpler methodology, note taking, would have worked as well or better.

How do we prevent behavior modeling from being used inappropriately? The easiest answer is to follow the decision flow chart outlined in Chapter 2 of this book. The challenge will be to utilize front-end analysis to make sure that behavior modeling is the appropriate technology. Overcome the urge to use behavior modeling simply for the sake of using it.

Ineffective Learning

The learning experience can become ineffective. One of the greatest dangers to behavior modeling is a departure from the basic, proven method for the sake of novelty. Many people in the training community like to change learning experiences to make them more interesting or exciting.

There have already been too many instances in which behavior-modeling learning designs have been so drastically modified that they do not provide all the learners with opportunities to skill practice, receive feedback, and build confidence through success experiences. We hear of situations in which only one out of three learners had an opportunity to skill practice or cases in which the feedback lowered the self-esteem and confidence of the learners.

Behavior modeling is vulnerable here because we can tamper with the learning experience without improving it. The strength of the classic behavior-modeling design is its simplicity. It is a simple, efficient way to learn. Yet, for some of us in the training community, behavior modeling may seem *too* simple; and we are tempted to liven it up, even though such embellishment may not improve learning effectiveness.

I am not saying that the behavior-modeling learning experience should not be changed. It should and will be changed, but these changes must be instituted thoughtfully after thorough field testing. Since its inception in the early Seventies, behavior modeling has changed significantly. In fact, the behavior-modeling learning experience of today enables managers to develop skills twice as fast as they could in the early Seventies. Nevertheless, we must make sure that changes increase, rather than hamper, the learning effectiveness.

Lack of Reinforcement

On-the-job reinforcement can be hindered. Behavior modeling greatly increases the learner's interactive skills. There is also substantial evidence that when those skills are not reinforced on the job, they will eventually be extinguished. The learner's immediate supervisor can have a significant impact on the learner's use of the skills and can act as a coach, a reinforcer, and a positive model.

Behavior modeling is vulnerable in this area because time pressure and resource shortage may eliminate management-reinforcement training. The high appeal of behavior modeling as a learning experience adds to the risk. For example, the managers in the classroom may be learning the skills extremely well. Their supervisors may be receiving good feedback about the training and thus do not feel a need to be involved. The bottom line would be enjoyable training that would not be reinforced and, therefore, that would have minimal impact on the organization.

The challenge to the training professionals is to examine the type of reinforcement needed by the learners and make sure that they receive it. A good way to check on this is to ask the learners for feedback on the reinforcement they are or are not receiving.

Lack of Intervention

A behavior-modeling program may be only training sessions, not an intervention. All the early applications of behavior modeling addressed specific needs that had been identified by management. At General Electric, management was concerned about the high turnover of its new employees (Burnaska, 1976). American Telephone & Telegraph (1975) wanted to improve supervisors' abilities to supervise the new work force. At Agway, management was concerned about the supervisors' ability to maintain a supportive and open work climate in its new semiautomated physical distribution centers.

Behavior-modeling training is vulnerable because it may be implemented without the full support of management. This has already happened in some organizations. Those who received training but not reinforcement have felt that the organization did not support the use of the new skills on the job. In most cases, this led to a high level of discontent among those trained and, ultimately, to the discontinuation of the behavior-modeling training.

The challenge to the training professional is to work with management to underscore the impact that behavior modeling can have on managers' skills and performance. He or she must work with management to identify problems that should be corrected or prevented. When management sees that a behavior-modeling program will have a positive impact on the organization, it will support the program.

THE SECOND DECADE

Behavior modeling's evolution will continue through its second decade. New needs for managers will surface; the organizations in which managers operate will become more complex; managers within organizations will become more diverse. All these changes will place new demands on management development and behavior modeling.

More Applications

Because of the increasing complexity and diversity of organizations and work groups, the future will hold opportunities for even more applications of behavior modeling. Behavior modeling is already being used to teach managers how to manage resources more effectively, implement productivity programs, and manage cost-reduction programs. In the near future, management-development programs may focus on the introduction of robots and other advanced technology into the work place, participation in community functions, and the need to interface with government officials.

The list is almost endless. Many of the potential uses for behavior modeling have not even been thought of yet. Not only will the applications be more varied, they will also involve a greater variety of managers. Behavior modeling may be used with senior managers to provide them with skills for teambuilding, working with the board of directors, and negotiating with various groups. Behavior modeling may also be used with middle managers to enable them to work more effectively in multinational organizations. It appears that there will be many novel applications for behavior modeling in the next decade.

More Complex Situations

Managers will be working in more complex environments. There will be more matrix organizations, with more managers as project team leaders and members. With the cost of transportation increasing dramatically and the cost of communications staying relatively constant, there will be more situations in which managers will interact via electronic communications. Multiparty interactions will become more common and complex. They will often electronically connect people in remote locations. Many interactions will require computers to feed data to the managers.

These interactions will require new and different skills for managers. Most likely, behavior modeling will be an appropriate learning technology for developing them.

Classroom situations will be considerably different, because they must replicate the real world. In multiparty interactions, for example, there may be a different set of critical steps for each member. These critical steps may include branching and recycling. The classroom may have a computer that interacts with the participants. In response to different sets of information supplied by a computer, they may be required to employ different combinations of interactive skills.

Whatever form the future takes, the expectation is that the learning experience will become more complex because the managers' environments and learning needs will become more complex.

Diagnostic Skills

In the Seventies, managers were equipped with skills enabling them to be more effective with members of their work groups. In the future, several sets of skills will be needed because of the diverse nature of the work group. The different categories of workers identified by Yankelovich (1979) will require managers to have several sets of skills. The same managerial skills will not be equally effective with the enterprising or aggressive person, the person who works for pleasure, the habitual worker, the professional middle manager, and the apathetic worker.

Managers will have to diagnose the types of peple they are interacting with and to select the appropriate skills to use. Therefore, the learning experience will first consist of developing diagnostic skills, then learning to use the skills that will be most effective for the situation.

In the future, managers will need many new skills, as well as the ability to decide when to use which skills with what individuals. The manager of the future must be able to diagnose a situation more accurately and to use the most appropriate skill. These needs can bring about drastic changes in the use of behavior modeling. The sheer complexity of future skill requirements makes us aware that training must be assimilated by managers more easily than ever before. Because managers have a limited amount of time, training in diagnostic and interactive skills must be time efficient.

New Hardware and Software

The coming years will produce rapidly changing technology.

Although about five hundred years elapsed between the invention of the Gutenberg press and the sound motion picture, only about fifty years elapsed between the sound motion picture and the introduction of microcomputers and videodiscs. New technology is impacting training at an overwhelming pace. When this is coupled with the increasing cost of transportation, we will see great changes taking place in managerial training.

No doubt all these new technologies will be incorporated into the behavior-modeling learning experience. Future behavior-modeling programs can be conducted with participants in separate geographical locations interconnected via electronic communication systems.

The use of branching programs, controlled by the minicomputer and videodisc, will allow instructors to demonstrate a model appropriate for specific types of workers. For example, the videodisc and minicomputer can store a variety of behaviors for each skill module. These behaviors can be put together in different configurations so that the most effective configurations can be demonstrated for specific workers.

Managers will need to combine interactive skills with noninteractive skills. For example, problem analysis has some interactive and some noninteractive elements. The interactive elements include fact finding with other individuals, whereas studying computer reports and other data exemplifies the noninteractive elements. Therefore, behavior modeling for interpersonal skills will be combined with behavior modeling for noninteractive skills.

The bottom line is that behavior modeling will be coupled with a growing number of technologies to produce a total learning experience. The interweaving of these different technologies into effective and exciting learning experiences will be tomorrow's challenge.

WHAT WILL REMAIN THE SAME?

If the future is going to bring about such drastic changes, then what elements of behavior modeling will remain the same? I believe that the following components of the behavior-modeling learning experience will remain much as they are today.

Well-Articulated Behavioral Objectives

One key to the success of behavior modeling has been its well-researched and field-tested instructional objectives. Program developers have taken the time to field test programs thoroughly before using them on a wide scale. The behavioral objectives have been specific and clear, and the behavior in each critical step has been well defined.

No matter how complex future interactions and future classroom sessions become, the need for well-articulated behavioral objectives will remain. The successful designers of future behavior-modeling programs will be those who complete the necessary research and field tests to assure that program objectives are based on the behavior that has been proven most effective.

Positive Model

A significant strength of behavior modeling is that it shows managers how to handle problem situations effectively. The modeling display provides managers with a *positive model* who is competent and effective in the use of specific, vividly displayed behaviors. The managers see the model manager accomplish his or her objective by following the critical steps and judiciously using generic skills.

As the future classroom includes more complex situations and as a greater variety of conditions affect those situations (such as greater diversity within work groups and the utilization of electronic homes for certain aspects of the work), there will still be a need for a positive model to show managers how to be effective in the more complex work environment. As new technology—including the videodisc, the micro-computer, and the satellite—provides numerous ways to display the model and to enable the learner to interact with the model, and as interactive and noninteractive modeling processes are combined, there will still be a need for a positive model.

Therefore, even if a manager watches a multiperson modeling display to learn both interactive and noninteractive skills, that manager must be able to identify with the positive model and conclude, "I can learn what that manager is doing."

In other words, there will always be a place for the competent and effective positive model to demonstrate those things that a manager must accomplish in real life.

Skill Practice

Behavior modeling has become widely used in part because—as the research demonstrates—managers will develop skills if they practice the skills and receive feedback.

Skill practice will continue to be an essential part of the behavior-modeling learning experience. Granted, some characteristics of the skill practice may change. It may be handled through electronic telecommunications between people in separate locations. The skill practice may be videotaped and the feedback handled one-on-one with the instructor. During the skill practice, the instructor may cue the video recorder to replay only the significant parts for the feedback session. The manner of feedback will most likely change significantly as the dynamics in the classroom change to include multiparty situations, diagnosis of the situation before the interaction, and data inputs from noninteractive sources. In any case, some type of skill practice and feedback will continue to be part of the learning experience.

Management Support and Reinforcement

As we look to the future, behavior modeling becomes more complex and involves more sophisticated and costly technologies. The investment in a behavior-modeling program will be much greater in the future. Then, even more than now, it will be imperative for behavior modeling to have a significant positive payoff for the organization. This cannot be accomplished without management support and reinforcement. Top managers will need to be tied directly into the design, development, and implementation of a behavior-modeling program. They will have to support it with the organization's resources and their personal endorsements. In addition, top managers will have to fulfill their roles as coaches, reinforcers, and positive models. The behavior-modeling program of the future will either have the active support of management or run a high risk of becoming just another expense—with little or no positive effect on the organization.

SUMMARY

The future for the use of behavior modeling in management development looks bright. Managers will need a greater variety of more sophisticated skills, and behavior modeling will be able to provide those skills by utilizing newly developed hardware and software and emerging technology.

For those just beginning to employ behavior-modeling technology, there is much to be learned and much to be accomplished. For those who are experienced in its use, the future promises a greater variety of sophisticated learning experiences, more challenges, and more satisfaction.

REFERENCES

American Telephone & Telegraph, Human Resources Development Department. Analysis and evaluation of supervisory relationships training (Internal report). New York: Author, 1975.

Burnaska, R.F. The effects of behavior modeling training upon managers' behaviors and employees' perceptions. *Personnel Psychology*, 1976, *29*(3), 329-335.

Robinson, J.C. Will behavior modeling survive the '80s? *Training and Development Journal*, 1980, *34*(1), 22-28.

Yankelovich, D. We need new motivational tools. *Industry Week*, August 6, 1979, pp. 61-68.

Glossary

Alternative positive behavior (APB)   A different and more effective way of performing a skill. An observer of a skill practice offers an APB by making a statement to the person who practiced the skill. The statement is always expressed in positive terms (i.e., "can do" rather than "should not do") and describes in behavioral terms what the learner can do to be more effective.

Andragogy   The science of adult learning.

Behavior modeling   A learning methodology that enables learners to develop specific skills and the confidence to use those skills by viewing a *model* who uses a specific set of steps in a defined situation, enacting the behaviors demonstrated by the model, then receiving feedback on their effectiveness.

Behavioral objectives   Statements of intended performance expressed in behavioral terms that will be the result of a *learning experience* and that indicate what the learner will be able to do as a result of the learning experience.

Competency   Skill or knowledge expressed in terms of observable behavior.

Content   The type of data used in a *learning experience*.

Contracting   See *contract learning*.

Contract learning   An agreement between a learner and an instructor (or other people) that specifies what skills the learner intends to gain, the learning resources he or she intends to use to gain them, and how he or she will demonstrate skill attainment.

Critical-incident analysis   A method of collecting data about incidents in which specific behaviors make the difference between success and failure in carrying out a specific function or job.

Critical steps   A check list of behaviors expressed succinctly and designed to guide the learner through an interaction. The critical steps are used by the learner both during the learning phase and during on-the-job application.

Educational hardware   Equipment designed for use by instructors and learners in conjunction with *educational software* to enable the learners to achieve their learning objectives (e.g., a videotape deck and monitor). Contrast *educational software.*

Educational software   Materials specifically developed for use by learners and instructors to enable the learner to achieve specific learning objectives (e.g., videotape cassette, workbook).

Error analysis   A method to determine the number of times that learners do *not* achieve specific *competencies.*

Field test   The evaluation of prototype materials in appropriate situations to determine necessary modifications.

Formative evaluation   Evaluation of instructional programs while they are still in the process of development.

Generic skills   Skills that are used by managers or supervisors in a variety of situations (e.g., listening skills or summarizing skills).

Intended outcomes   The results expected from a *learning experience* or training program. Intended outcomes are often expressed as *instructional objectives.*

Interactive skills   Skills used by managers or supervisors as they interact with other people. These skills include both verbal and nonverbal components.

Instructional objectives   Statements of the *intended outcomes* of a *learning experience* expressed in terms of what the learner will know, feel, or be able to do as a result of that learning experience.

Learned helplessness   The result of a *learning experience* in which the learner determines that he or she cannot master a certain *competency.*

Learning experience   An event during which a person gains new knowledge, skills, or awareness.

Management reinforcement   A method by which managers sustain their subordinates' use of skills learned in a workshop or training program (see *reinforcement*).

Management-reinforcement workshop   A workshop in which managers learn why it is important for them to reinforce the skills learned by their subordinate supervisors and in which managers develop the skills necessary for *reinforcement.*

Model   The person in a *modeling display* who demonstrates how to handle specific situations.

Modeling display   The entire vignette in which a *model* handles a defined situation by using the specific skills to be learned by the viewer. The modeling display is typically a film or videotape.

Overlearning   Additional acquisition of knowledge or skill after the learner has demonstrated *competency* in that knowledge or skill.

Patterned interview   An interview in which the interviewer uses a predetermined sequence of questions to obtain information from the interviewee.

Pedagogy   The science of teaching children.

Peer reinforcement   *Reinforcement* that managers or supervisors receive from their peer managers or supervisors in the organization.

Process   The events or activities that take place during a *learning experience*.

Program developer   The individual who designs *learning experiences* to accomplish specific *instructional objectives* and who prepares the appropriate *educational software*.

Reinforcement   A process by which some stimulus, occurring after a response or activity, increases the rate at which that response or activity occurs in a standard situation. This increases the probability that the response or activity will reoccur when the situation reoccurs.

Situational skills   Skills that pertain to specific managerial or supervisory situations, such as "handling employee complaints" or "improving employee work habits."

Skill areas   Broad categories of job-related behaviors that, when used by the learner on the job, will enable him or her to handle a specific situation successfully.

Skill mastery   A predetermined level of skill development that will enable the learner to handle the *skill area* successfully.

Skill module   The classroom session that enables a learner to develop the needed skills and confidence for a specific *skill area*.

Skill practice   A learning exercise, similar to a role play, whereby the learner can practice the skills previously demonstrated by the *model*.

Summative evaluation   Evaluation intended to provide data about the effectiveness of a training program.

Target audience   Those individuals in an organization toward whom a *learning experience* is directed and for whom a training program is conducted.

Training manager or training director   The primary staff person responsible for the development of skills and knowledge among employees, supervisors, and managers within an organization.

Appendix A

PATTERNED INTERVIEW: SUPERVISORS IN UNION ENVIRONMENTS

Introduction

I am a Consultant/Program Developer with Development Dimensions International, a firm which is located in Pittsburgh, Pennsylvania, and develops training programs. At this time, I am gathering information from supervisors about what they do in handling situations which involve a union representative. This information will be used in developing supervisory training programs, tailored to the specific needs of supervisors who work in companies which have unions. This information will help us use the "real world" approach in building the programs. Our objectives in talking with you are:

A. to learn about your job as a supervisor;

B. to talk about some specific aspects of your job;

C. to get your ideas on how to handle situations that involve the union representative.

Information you share with me will be completely confidential. This information will be tabulated in with responses from other supervisors (from other organizations). I'll be asking questions and making notes so that I don't lose the highlights of your answers. You can certainly see anything I write down if you wish. Do you have any questions before we begin?

1. Since I know very little about your job, can you tell me what your current job responsibilities are?

2. How long have you been in your present position? What other work experience have you had?

   What supervisory and management training have you had?

3. How many employees report to you?

   What positions do they have?

---

4. I would like to talk about your method of dealing with employee grievances. What types of grievances have been brought to you in the past year?

   What are the most frequent kinds of grievances?

   What are the most difficult to handle? Why?

5. Tell me about a situation in which a grievance was brought to you involving an issue other than discipline or a formal warning.

   a. What was the situation?

   b. Who was present in the discussion?

   c. What was actually said in the discussion?

   How did you start the conversation?

   What did the employee say?

   What did the union representative say?

   How was the grievance described?

   What questions did you ask as you gathered facts about the situation?

   What information did you obtain?

   What did you say was your position?

   What part of the contract did you quote or how did you describe it? (Did you actually pull the contract out and quote verbatim?)

   Were you able to resolve the grievance in the first meeting?

   If not, what did you do next?

   If yes, what agreement was reached?

   What were the immediate results? Long-term results?

   Was the discussion documented? If so, in what way?

6. Describe a grievance situation you had to handle in which, after the grievance was brought to you, you had to further investigate the situation.

   a. What was the situation?

   b. Who did you talk to to get more information?

   c. What questions did you ask?

   d. What information did you get?

7. Think of a situation in which you discussed a grievance with your manager (boss) to get more information.

   What was the situation?

   What did you say? What questions did you ask?

   What did your manager say?

   What suggestions did your manager make as to how you should handle the grievance?

8. In handling grievances, what help do you usually get when you discuss the grievance with your manager?

   What benefit is this to you?

9. Please give me an example of a time when you had a second meeting on the same grievance in which you attempted to resolve the grievance on your own level.

   a. Think of a situation in which you were successful in resolving the grievance at your own level.

   What was the situation?

   Who was present in the discussion?

   Describe what you said.

   What did the employee say?

   What did the union representative say?

   What did you say was your position?

   What part of the contract did you quote and how did you describe it? (Did you actually pull the contract out?)

   How was the grievance resolved?

   What were the immediate results? Long-term results?

   Was the discussion documented? If so, how?

   b. Tell me about a situation in which you were not able to resolve the grievance at your own level.

   What was the situation?

   Who was present in the discussion?

   What did you say?

   What did the employee say?

   What did the union representative say?

   What did you say was your position?

   What part of the contract did you quote and how did you describe it? (Did you actually pull the contract out?)

   At what level was the grievance finally resolved? How?

   Was the discussion documented? If so, how?

10. Tell me about a problem that you discussed with an employee which resulted in an employee grievance.

    a. What was the situation?

    b. Who was present in the discussion?

    c. What did you say in describing the problem?

    d. What did the employee say?

    e. What did the union representative say? (if appropriate)

    f. What did you say was your position?

    g. Were disciplinary procedures discussed? How?

    h. What was the employee's reaction?

    i. What follow-up action was agreed to?

    j. Was the discussion documented? If so, in what way?

11. Describe a time when you terminated or attempted to terminate an employee.
    a. What was the problem?
    b. What was the employee's:
       Position/job grade?
       Seniority?
       Performance rating?
    c. Had you had previous discussions about the problem?
       How many?
       Over what period of time?
       Nature of the discussions?
       Were disciplinary procedures discussed? How?
    d. Who was present in the termination meeting?
    e. What was actually said?
       How did you start the discussion?
       What did the employee say?
       What did the union representative say?
    f. What reasons did you give for the termination?
       How did the employee react?
       How did the union representative react?
    g. What was the outcome of the meeting?
    h. Was the discussion documented? If so, how?

12. When you discuss a performance problem or a poor work habit with an employee for the first time, is the union representative present?
    In every case?
    Under what circumstances?
    Is the discussion documented? If so, in what way?

13. What part does your manager generally play in handling grievances?
    What are the benefits of your manager's participation?
    What areas that involve your manager's participation could be improved? How?

14. Describe a situation where you participated in a grievance meeting with your manager.
    a. What was the situation?
    b. Who was involved in the meeting?
    c. What was said?
    d. How was the situation resolved?
    e. Was the meeting documented? If so, how?
    f. What were the immediate results? Long term results?

15. How often does your manger praise you for resolving a grievance?
    Give me an example of a time when this occurred.

    a. What was the situation?

    b. What did your manager say?

    c. How did you feel?

16. Can you show me an example of the documentation for a recent grievance situation?

17. Are there any situations we haven't talked about that would involve the union representative? If so, what are they? How often do they occur?

18. What is the most difficult part of supervising within a contractual environment?

19. The object of the next question is to find out what kinds of training (that may or may not exist) supervisors would find useful to help them become more effective on the job. What kind of training would you find useful?

20. Are there any questions I can answer for you?

    Closing

Thank you very much for your time and help. Your responses will be quite useful in helping us make our supervisory-training programs more relevant to the "real world."

Appendix B

ADDITIONAL RESEARCH STUDIES
ON BEHAVIOR MODELING

Eleven studies are summarized, and the results are presented in a graphic form. This information should aid training directors in developing, implementing, and evaluating behavior-modeling programs for managers and supervisors so they can develop skills and use them on the job.

Organization: Agway Inc.
     Syracuse, New York

Experimental Design: Patterned interviews were conducted with subordinates of supervisors before the supervisors were trained in behavior modeling and six months after training to determine how effectively the supervisors handled nine specific employee situations.

Type of Measurement: Behavior

Date Completed: 1973

Results:

**Effectiveness in Resolving Critical Situations After Supervisory Training
(As Perceived by Employees)**

	No. of Situations
More Effective Resolution	7
No Change	2
Total	9

Number of supervisors = 6

Source of data: Unpublished study by Agway Inc., Syracuse, N.Y., 1973.

Organization: Agway Inc.
                               Syracuse, New York

Experimental Design: Data on the way supervisors handled interpersonal
                               situations were collected from the subordinates of
                               supervisors in an accounting department before the
                               supervisors were trained in interaction management
                               and seven months after they completed the training.
                               Data were also obtained from subordinates of a control
                               group.

Type of Measurement: Behavior

Date Completed: 1975

Results:

Differences in Percentage of Employee Responses About Supervisors' Use of Skills on the Job

Skill Area	Pre[1]	Post[1]	Difference	Control[2]	Trained[1]	Difference
Orienting a New Employee	31%	54%	+23	48%	54%	+6
Overcoming Resistance to Change	24%	60%	+36	24%	60%	+36
Reducing Absenteeism	60%	86%	+26	69%	86%	+17
Handling Emotional Situations	53%	68%	+15	46%	68%	+22
Using Effective Follow-Up Action	28%	43%	+15	37%	43%	+7
Teaching an Employee a New Task	54%	65%	+11	52%	65%	+13
Reducing Tardiness	50%	66%	+16	46%	66%	+20
Handling Employee Complaints	54%	67%	+13	60%	67%	+7
Improving Employee Performance	80%	80%	0	63%	80%	+17
Delegating Responsibility	35%	30%	-5	39%	30%	-9

[1]Number of supervisors = 8; number of employees = 19
[2]Number of supervisors = 8; number of employees = 24

Reprinted by permission from W.C. Byham, D. Adams, and A. Kiggins. Transfer of Modeling Training to the Job. *Personnel Psychology*, 1976, *29*(3), p. 348. Copyright © 1976 by *Personnel Psychology*.

Organization: American Telephone & Telegraph Company
                             New York, New York

Experimental Design: Training-effects data on supervisors' performance were
                             collected from course instructors during the training,
                             from questionnaires completed by the supervisors at the
                             conclusion of the training, and from private in-depth
                             interviews with the supervisors three months after
                             the training.

Type of Measurement: Reaction (Figure A)
                             Behavior (Figures B and C)
                             Results (See Table 10, Chapter 11.)

Date Completed: 1975

Results:

Useful	91%
Not Useful	9%

Number of supervisors = 44

**Figure A. Supervisors' Perceptions of Usefulness of Training
Three Months After Training**

Used Training	82%
Not Used	18%

Number of supervisors = 44

Figure B. Application of Training Within Three Months After Training

More Discussions	59%
Same Number of Discussions	41%

Number of supervisors = 44

**Figure C. Frequency of Supervisor-Initiated Discussions
with Subordinates Since Training**

Source of data for Figures A, B, and C: American Telephone & Telegraph, Human
Resources Development Department. *Analysis and Evaluation of Supervisory Relationships Training* (Internal report). New York: Author, 1975.

Organization:	Central Telephone Company
	Lincoln, Nebraska
Experimental Design:	Supervisors were videotaped while handling three simulated employee interactions both before starting and after completing training in interaction management. The videotaped situations were then evaluated in terms of the supervisors' overall effectiveness in resolving the problem situations and in terms of eight supervisory dimensions.
Type of Measurement:	Learning
Date Completed:	1975
Results:	

Overall Ratings of Trained Supervisors' Effectiveness in Simulated Situations

Overall Rating	Before	After
Excellent	0%	17%
Above Average	22%	25%
Average	39%	58%
Below Average	17%	0%
Poor	22%	0%

[a]Number of supervisors = 18
[b]Number of supervisors = 12

Average Ratings[a] by Dimension and Overall Effectiveness

Dimension	Before[b]	After[c]	Difference
Sensitivity	3.4	3.9	+0.5
Management Control	3.1	3.6	+0.5
Judgment	2.9	3.2	+0.3
Listening Skill	3.2	4.0	+0.8
Flexibility	2.5	3.4	+0.9
Problem Analysis	2.6	3.7	+1.1
Oral Presentation Skill	3.1	3.5	+0.4
Leadership	2.5	3.7	+1.2
OVERALL EFFECTIVENESS	2.61	3.58	+0.97

[a]Rating Scale: 1 = Poor/Low
     2 = Below Average
     3 = Average
     4 = Above Average
     5 = Excellent/High
[b]Number of supervisors = 18
[c]Number of supervisors = 12

Source of data for preceding tables: Unpublished study by Central Telephone Company, Lincoln, Nebraska, 1975.

Organization: Lukens Steel Company
Coatesville, Pennsylvania

Experimental Design: Supervisors in both the trained group and the control group were rated before and after the interaction-management training on their handling of three simulated problem discussions.

Type of Measurement: Learning

Date Completed: 1976

Results:

Assessed Skill Level After Training
(Based on Performance in Simulations)

Assessed Skill Level	Trained	Control
Excellent or Above Average	58%	21%
Average	21%	37%
Below Average or Poor	21%	42%
	100%	100%

Number of trained supervisors = 24
Number of control supervisors = 8

Source of data: H.D. King & C.G. Arlinghaus. Interaction Management Validated in the Steel Industry. *Assessment and Development,* 1976, *3*(2), 1-2.

Organization:	Rhodesian National Railways
	Salisbury and Bulawayo, Rhodesia
Experimental Design:	Pretest information was collected on a questionnaire from supervisors in both the trained and control groups just before interaction-management training. Seven months later, post-test data were collected on the same questionnaire from both groups of supervisors.
Type of Measurement:	Behavior
Date Completed:	1976
Results:	

Percentage Changes in Supervisors' Reactions to Employee Problems

Number of Times	Poor Employee Performance		Poor Employee Work Habits		Poor Employee Attendance	
	Trained[1]	Control[2]	Trained[1]	Control[2]	Trained[1]	Control[2]
Problem Causing Supervisor Concern	10%	2%	14%	4%	80%	(5)%[3]
Problem Occurring "More Than Once a Week"	50	0	90	50	60	0
Problem Tackled "Every Time It Occurs"	(20)[3]	0	5	0	7	(5)[3]
Problem Showing "Considerable Improvement"	50	0	30	0	100	10
Problem Handled in a "Very Confident" Manner	33	6	100	25	50	6

[1]Number of supervisors = 12
[2]Number of supervisors = 6
[3]Numbers in brackets reflect a change in an undesired direction.

Reprinted by permission from A. Petasis. Behaviour Modelling: It Can Be an Efficient Training Tool. *People & Profits,* 1977, *4*(11), p. 9.

Percentage Changes in Supervisors' Styles in Handling Employee Problems

Supervision Index	Trained	Control
Participative	5%	(7%)[3]
Authoritarian	60%	2%
Inactive	73%	0

Number of trained supervisors = 12
Number of control supervisors = 6
Number in brackets reflects a change in an undesired direction.

Source of data: See footnote for preceding table.

Characteristics of Trained and Control Groups

Characteristics	Trained[1]	Control[2]
Age	47 yrs.	49 yrs.
Length of Service in the Organization	22 yrs.	22 yrs.
Supervisory Experience in the Organization	2.7 yrs.	3.2 yrs.
European Employees Under Supervisor	15	15
African Employees Under Supervisor	27	35

[1]Number of supervisors = 12
[2]Number of supervisors = 6

Reprinted by permission from A. Petasis, p. 3. See footnote for preceding table.

Organization: Medical Group Management Association

Experimental Design: Supervisors completed a questionnaire both before and
                         immediately after behavior-modeling training, and, in
                         the 1977 group, again eight months after training. The
                         scores on these self-evaluations were used as a measure
                         of supervisors' self-confidence in handling specific
                         supervisory problems. In addition, the administrators
                         of the supervisors in the 1977 sessions completed a
                         comparable questionnaire both before and eight months
                         after training as a measure of the supervisors' job
                         performance.

Type of Measurement: Learning
                         Behavior (See Table 8 in Chapter 1.)

Date Completed: 1976 and 1977

Results:

Mean Self-Ratings of Supervisory Ability in 22 Areas[1]

Area of Supervision	1976[2]			1977[3]			8 Months Later[4]
	Pre	Program[5]	Post	Pre	Program[5]	Post	
Administering Discipline	9.42	T	10.73	6.25	D	8.93	8.49
Following-up Lack of Improvement	10.56	D	12.00	7.10	T	9.83	9.56
Dealing with Performance Problems	10.42	T	12.11	7.89	T	9.95	10.01
Handling Discrimination Complaints	10.52	N	11.71				
Reducing Tardiness	11.14	N	13.61	7.83	N	10.41	9.90

[1]Rating scale: 3 (low) to 15 (high)
[2]Number of supervisors = 125
[3]Number of supervisors = 110
[4]Number of supervisors = 71
[5]T = Trained with skill-practice session
D = Discussed but not trained
N = Neither discussed nor trained

Reprinted by permission from T.J. DeHaan, G.C. Thornton III, and D.A. Waldman. Supervisory Training Produces Positive Changes in Self-Confidence and Job Performance. *Medical Group Management*, 1979, p. 30.

Mean Self-Ratings (continued)

Dealing with Poor Work Habits	11.23	T	12.46	8.01	T	10.20	9.88
Handling Employee Complaints	11.26	T	12.24	8.65	T	10.32	10.77
Setting Goals	11.32	N	12.37	7.68	N	9.90	9.87
Handling Emotional Situations	10.32	T	11.57	8.08	N	9.82	10.17
Overcoming Resistance to Change	11.34	N	12.44	8.99	N	10.61	11.07
Dealing with Physicians				8.33	T	9.91	10.10
Motivating the Average Performer	11.53	T	12.59	8.44	D	10.44	10.46
Discussing Problems Between Departments				8.51	T	10.62	10.64
Improving Attendance	11.35	N	13.51				
Handling Client Complaints	11.36	T	12.27	9.03	T	10.61	10.79
Reviewing Performance	11.72	N	12.00				
Solving Problems in a Work Group				8.70	T	10.79	10.93
Motivating the Long-Term Employee				8.98	T	10.71	10.97
Teaching an Employee a New Job	11.87	T	12.87	9.40	N	10.78	11.29
Maintaining Improved Performance	11.96	D	13.08	8.58	D	10.75	10.59
Delegating Responsibility	11.96	T	12.66	9.11	N	10.74	11.04
Orienting the New Employee	12.41	N	14.19				

Organization:	Norden Laboratories, Inc.
	Lincoln, Nebraska
Experimental Design:	A survey questionnaire focusing on the current performance of supervisors was completed both before and after interaction-management training by supervisors in a trained group and a control group and also by their managers and subordinates. In addition, supervisors in both the trained group and the control group were videotaped while handling a simulated employee interaction before and after interaction-management training. The videotaped situations were then evaluated in terms of five dimensions and the supervisors' overall effectiveness in handling the situation.
Type of Measurement:	Learning (See table on supervisors' skills.)
	Behavior (See table on supervisory behavior.)
Date Completed:	1978
Results:	

Average Ratings of Supervisors' Skill in Handling Supervisory Assignments

		Pre-Test				Post-Test		
Ratings by	N^a	Control	N^a	Trained	N^a	Control	N^a	Trained
Subordinates	57	2.99	76	2.80	39	2.87	51	2.74
Self	12	3.21	11	3.01	10	3.18	11	3.21
Managers	11	3.07	12	3.05	10	2.96	9	3.21
Overall		3.03		2.85		2.94		2.87

^{a}N = Number of respondents to survey questionnaire

Average Ratings of Supervisory Behavior in Simulated Situations

	Pre-Test		Post-Test	
Dimension	Control	Trained	Control	Trained
Sensitivity	2.50	2.48	1.92	2.24
Listening	2.56	2.54	2.31	2.82
Problem Analysis	2.44	2.15	2.03	2.48
Problem Solving	2.42	2.00	2.06	2.48
Leadership/Control	2.53	1.94	2.08	2.73
OVERALL EFFECTIVENESS	2.53	2.30	2.11	2.61

Number of control supervisors = 12
Number of trained supervisors = 11

Source of data for preceding tables: J.P. Judt. *An Evaluation of First-Line Supervisor Skill Training.* Unpublished master's thesis, University of Nebraska, 1978.

| *Organization:* | Weyerhaeuser Company |
| | Aberdeen, Washington |

Experimental Design: A reaction questionnaire was administered to supervisors who participated in the behavior-modeling training immediately after training and again eight months later. Supervisors in both the trained group and the control group were videotaped while handling a simulated employee interaction three months after training, and they also completed a learning measures test containing eighty-five situational questions six months after training. In addition, superintendents evaluated the job performance of supervisors in both the trained and control groups one month before training and again one year after training, using behavioral-observation scales and the company's traditional performance-appraisal instrument.

Type of Measurement: Reaction (See table on supervisors' reactions.)
Learning (See tables on supervisors' effectiveness and performance.)
Behavior (See Table 7 in Chapter 11.)

Date Completed: 1978

Results:

Average Ratings of Supervisors' Reactions to Training

	Average Ratings	
Reaction Measures	Immediately After Training	8 Months After Training
Extent to Which Training Helped You Do the Job Better	4.5	4.6
Extent to Which Training Helped You Interact More Effectively with:		
(a) Employees	4.5	4.6
(b) Peers	3.2	3.7
(c) Supervisors	3.8	4.2
Degree to Which You Would Recommend This Training to Other Supervisors	4.9	4.9

Number of supervisors = 20
Five-point rating scale

Overall Ratings of Supervisors' Effectiveness
in Simulated Situations Three Months After Training

Group	Overall Rating
Trained[a]	4.11
Control (with learning points)[b]	2.70
Control (without learning points)[c]	2.84

Five-point rating scale

---

[a]Number of supervisors = 20
[b]Number of supervisors = 10
[c]Number of supervisors = 10

Overall Ratings of Supervisors' Performance
on Learning Measures Test Six Months After Training

Group	Overall Rating
Trained	301.00
Control	273.36

Number of trained supervisors = 20
Number of control supervisors = 20
425-point rating scale

Source of data for three preceding tables: G.P. Latham & L.M. Saari. Application of Social Learning Theory to Training Managers through Behavior Modeling. *Journal of Applied Psychology*, 1979, *64*(3), 239-246.

Organization:	Orange County HSA/Social Services Staff Development Division Santa Ana, California
Experimental Design:	A questionnaire to measure supervisors' perceptions of their own skills in handling employee problems was administered to supervisors both before and after participating in interaction-management (IM) training. Also IM-trained managers completed a questionnaire on the effectiveness of IM skills and the degree to which the skills were used by their subordinates.
Type of Measurement:	Learning (See table on supervisors' perceptions.) Behavior (See table on managers' ratings.)
Date Completed:	1979
Results:	

Supervisors' Perceptions of Their Skills in Handling Employee Problems

Group	Pre-test	Post-test
Group 1	79.4	85.5
Group 2a	78.5	82.2
Group 2b	—	80.9
Combined Group 2a & 2b	—	81.5

Number of Group 1 supervisors = 25
Number of Group 2 supervisors = 31

Managers' Ratings of Supervisors' Effectiveness and Use of IM Skills on the Job

	Managers' Ratings		
Questions	Yes	No	Not Applicable
Are Supervisors Using IM Skills?	8	2	—
Have Supervisors' Job Performances Improved?	8	—	2
Are Managers Using Reinforcement Skills?	8	—	2

Number of managers = 10

Source of data for preceding tables: F. Carillo. A Report on the Evaluation of the Interaction Management Program (Internal report). Santa Ana, CA: Orange County HSA/Social Services Staff Development Division, 1979.

Organization: University of Chicago Hospitals and Clinics

Experimental Design: A training-impact-auditing session was conducted with supervisors and managers who had participated in the interaction-management (IM) training to explore the achieved results and unachieved goals. Structured interviews were also conducted with supervisors and managers who had participated in the IM program 60 to 180 days after the completion of the training to evaluate on-the-job changes in supervisors' behaviors that could be attributed to IM training and the impact of those changes on the work area.

Type of Measurement: Behavior
Results (See Table 9 in Chapter 11.)

Date Completed: 1979

Results:

Achieved Results (in Rank Order)

1. Confidence in supervisory role
2. Constructive employee discussions
3. Better team work among many peer supervisors
4. More successful implementation of change
5. Improved work-group performance
6. Improved employee attitudes and morale
7. Effective delegation: manager to supervisor; supervisor to subordinate
8. Complaint handling

Unachieved Goals

1. Management of some extremely difficult employees
2. Comprehension of UCHC personnel policies and procedures
3. Motivation of the "good" employee
4. Specific skills in union relations
5. Motivation in work areas perceived to need supervisory training to participate in the program
6. Other supervisory skills, e.g., job training, job-applicants interviewing, time management, and patient relations

Figure D. Results of Interaction-Management Training

Supervisors' Self-Ratings of Overall Job Behavior After Interaction-Management Training

Job Behavior	Supervisors' Ratings			
	Better	No Change	Worse	Don't Know
Self-Confidence in Supervisory Role	26	0	0	0
Communicating with Subordinates	22	4	0	0
Communicating with Superiors	9	13	2	2
Awareness of Individual Needs and Differences	24	2	0	0
Receptiveness of Ideas of Others in Problem Solving	23	3	0	0
Promptness and Timeliness in Handling Employee Situations	22	3	1	0
Identifying with Management and Organizational Objectives	13	11	0	2
Giving Orders	19	7	0	0
Introducing Change	21	3	0	2
Appraising Employee Performance and Work Habits	20	6	0	0
Handling Complaints and Grievances	22	3	0	1
Delegating	17	9	0	0
Planning Important Discussions	23	2	0	1

Number of supervisors = 26

Source of data for preceding figure and table: J. Nicholson. *Interaction Management Supervisory Training Evaluation Study.* Unpublished study, University of Chicago Hospitals and Clinics, 1979.

Bibliography

Adams, D., & Kiggins, A. Transfer of interaction-modeling training to the job—New research results. *Assessment & Development*, 1976, 3(1), 1; 5-6.

The authors discuss the experimental design used in a research study conducted by Agway Inc. and present the results of the study. This new evidence confirms that on-the-job behavior is changed as a consequence of interaction-modeling training.

American Telephone & Telegraph, Human Resources Development Department. *Analysis and evaluation of Supervisory Relationships Training* (Internal report). New York: Author, 1975.

Focusing on the evaluative criteria of (1) relevance to job situation, (2) effectiveness of training, (3) transfer and application to job situation, (4) acceptance by trainees, and (5) worth of program in terms of actual impact and benefits, this report provides a thorough analysis and evaluation of AT&T's Supervisory Relationships Training (SRT) program. The findings indicated that SRT was an effective training program that increased first-level supervisors' skills in dealing with problems they faced on the job. It also indicated that once trained, supervisors frequently applied their increased knowledge and skills to their job situations.

American Telephone & Telegraph Company, Management Selection and Development Research, Human Resources Development Department. Supervisory Relationships Training. *A new approach to supervisory training: Results of evaluation research*. New York: Author, 1974.

After briefly describing AT&T's Supervisory Relationships Training (SRT) program, this report presents detailed information on the manner in which SRT was evaluated and the results that were obtained at Pacific Telephone & Telegraph and Illinois Bell. The research findings indicate that the overall performance of supervisors trained in SRT was dramatically superior to that of untrained supervisors in simulated problem-centered discussions.

An achievement plan that produces measurable results—PRODPLAN. *A.B.T.A. Businessman's Journal*, 1979, 2(1), 11-14.

This article describes a newly developed behavior-modeling program in Australia—PRODPLAN. PRODPLAN provides supervisors with the techniques to implement a practical productivity project. The program gives employees the chance to contribute to the overall productivity of the company by finding sources of wasted energy, materials, etc., in the place where they work.

Are you an andragog? *IM Navigator*, 1977, *1*(1), 1-2.

This article briefly describes five basic assumptions that are made about the learning process in andragogy (the teaching of adults) that differ from those of pedagogy (the teaching of children). It then discusses the ways in which interaction management builds on these basic assumptions of the andragogical model for learning.

Behavior modeling. *Bulletin on Training*, 1976, *1*(3), 3.

This article briefly describes the major components of the behavior-modeling approach to training: (1) provision of models, (2) tryout of behavior, (3) positive reinforcement, and (4) transfer of training.

Behavior modeling: When to use it? *IM Navigator*, 1980, *4*(1), 1-2; 19.

This article answers the questions "Can behavior modeling be used in any training situation?" and "If not, what criteria should one use to determine whether behavior modeling is appropriate for a given situation?" Eight major questions for deciding whether or not to use behavior modeling are discussed.

Behaviour modelling: A new approach to supervisory training. *People & Profits*, 1975, *2*(11), 28-31.

This article, the first in a five-part series, briefly introduces the concept of behavior modeling as a new training technique. It suggests that as a training method, behavior modeling has a wide application in industry, particularly for training supervisors in interpersonal skills.

Bruno, A.L. *A study of behavioral principles applied to the training of supervisors.* Unpublished master's thesis, University of West Florida, 1975.

This thesis is a detailed study of interaction-modeling techniques in two organizations. The article describes the perceptions of the trainees (thirteen supervisors), three managers, and six trainers. The study provides considerable information about interaction modeling based on the perceptions of those interviewed. In addition, highlights of AT&T's program are discussed. The study indicates that the interaction-modeling process is a valuable addition to supervisory training.

Burnaska, R.F. The effects of behavior modeling training upon managers' behaviors and employees' perceptions. *Personnel Psychology*, 1976, *29*(3), 329-335.

This paper describes the evaluation study that was conducted at General Electric to determine if the interpersonal skills of managers who were trained through behavior-modeling techniques improved, how long the effects of the training could be expected to last, and if employees of the trained managers could perceive changes in their managers' overall behaviors. Although the research indicates that the managers' interpersonal skills improved significantly after training (with even greater improvement occurring four months after the training), employees' perceptions of their managers' overall behaviors indicated only slight improvement.

Byham, W.C., Adams, D., & Kiggins, A. Transfer of modeling training to the job. *Personnel Psychology*, 1976, *29*(3), 345-349.

This paper describes the interaction-management training program used at Agway Inc. and how it particularly focused on transfer of training to the job. Some preliminary research findings indicating the effectiveness of the transfer of training are presented.

Byham, W.C., & Robinson, J.C. Interaction Management: Supervisory training that changes job performance. *Personnel Administrator*, 1976, *21*(2), 16-19.

The authors describe how the Interaction Management (training) System was designed to overcome the traditional barriers that inhibit transfer of training from the classroom to the work setting. They propose that the Interaction Management System—by focusing on specific needs of supervisors, skill development, confidence building, on-the-job applications, and peer and management reinforcement—can and will change on-the-job behavior of supervisors.

Byham, W., & Robinson, J. Interaction modeling: A new concept in supervisory training. *Training and Development Journal*, 1976, *30*(2), 20-33.

Using the Interaction Management (training) System as an example, the authors describe the elements of a typical interaction-modeling program. They also review a number of the validation studies that demonstrate that supervisors are able to handle problem situations with employees more effectively when they have been trained in programs utilizing interaction-modeling techniques. Program design and the role of the classroom administrator in interaction-modeling programs are also discussed.

Byham, W.C., & Robinson, J. Building supervisory confidence—A key to transfer of training. *Personnel Journal*, 1977, *56*(5), 248-250; 253.

The authors emphasize that an effective transfer of training requires supervisors not only to develop new skills, but also to build confidence that they can successfully utilize those skills in on-the-job situations. They then describe how supervisory confidence is built in the Interaction Management System through the use of positive reinforcement.

Cook, D.D. Foremen: Where theory collides with reality. *Industry Week*, April 6, 1971, pp. 74-80.

This article indicates that today's supervisors are neither workers nor managers and that they are ill-equipped to handle the jobs they are being asked to do. The reasons are (1) supervisors' responsibilities and authority are unclear, (2) methods of selecting supervisors are inadequate, (3) the training development of supervisors is inadequate, and (4) supervisors' compensations are too low. The article cites three organizations that have overcome supervisory ineffectiveness through improved training and selection.

Cushing, D. When and how to use incentives in training. *Training*, April 1981, pp. 57-66.

The article describes several organizations that have used incentives in conjunction with training programs to improve performance. One pharmaceutical company improved quality (1) by providing all employees with the opportunity to compete for a weekly incentive prize, (2) by offering training in human relations skills to supervisors, and (3) by implementing a cost-reduction suggestion program. Another organization is comparing three different types of training: (1) without incentives, (2) with a single management-selected incentive, and (3) with incentives selected by the trainees. The organizations have incentive programs with nonmonetary rewards. In all instances, supervisory training was suggested as an important element in boosting performance.

Daniels, W.R. How to make and evaluate video models. *Training and Development Journal*, 1981, *35*(12), 31-33.

The author explains the effectiveness of videotaped modeling displays in behavior-modeling programs and discusses the possible hazards of misusing them. He offers a set of criteria for developing a "pure, focused" modeling display. The article also includes a thorough check list for evaluating and perfecting videotaped displays.

DeHaan, T.J., Thornton, G.C., & Waldman, D.A. Supervisory training produces positive changes in self-confidence and job performance. *Medical Group Management*, March/April 1979, pp. 28-32.

This article explains the special supervisory-training needs of the medical profession and, subsequently, outlines the method and program utilized in training medical-group-practice supervisors. The authors focus on an evaluation study conducted before and after the supervisors received supervisory training targeted to their specific needs. Supervisors trained in behavior modeling showed a positive increase in their self-confidence and ability to handle supervisor-employee discussions and were rated higher on performance appraisals after training than before training.

Enhancing management skill. *Chain Store Age Executive*, November 1977, pp. 38; 43.

This article briefly discusses the increasing popularity of behavior-modeling training among various retail chains and some of the positive results that have been achieved.

Gaines, D.L., & Salmon, W.A. Does what you do make a difference? Prove it! *Journal of Bank Training*, 1979, *1*(1), 17-21

The authors describe the results of the Interaction Management System in the Girard Bank. They explain how they attempted to answer the following questions in their evaluation study: (1) Is there bottom-line impact? (2) Did changes occur in the participants' management behaviors? (3) Did their attitudes change?

Gannon, J.S. How to handle discipline within the new National Labor Relations Board requirements. *Personnel Administrator*, March 1981, pp. 43-47.

The author references several recent decisions by the National Labor Relations Board, indicating that in fact-finding discussions that may lead to disciplinary action, the employee has the right to be represented by a third party. Under these circumstances, the supervisor must be prepared to deal with both the employee and the third party—who most likely will be a union representative and an advocate for the employee. In non-fact-finding discussions, in which a supervisor is communicating disciplinary action to the employee, the third party need *not* be present. The author indicates that supervisors need a high level of interpersonal skills to handle these types of discussions and recommends behavior modeling for developing these skills.

Goldstein, A.P. Increasing skill transfer. *IM Navigator*, 1978, *2*(1), 1-2.

This article is a synopsis of a keynote address at the second annual Advanced Conference on Interaction Modeling. Goldstein points out that the real issue in any type of training is not whether the learners acquire the skills, but whether new skills are transferred to the job. Several principles of transfer enhancement are discussed.

Goldstein, A.P., & Sorcher, M. Changing managerial behavior by applied learning techniques. *Training and Development Journal*, 1973, *27*(3), 36-39.

The authors propose that the major weakness in most management training is an unnecessary concern with attitude change as opposed to behavior change. As an alternative, they offer a behaviorally oriented training paradigm based on the principles of contemporary learning theory.

Goldstein, A.P., & Sorcher, M. *Changing supervisor behavior*. New York: Pergamon Press, 1974.

This book details a training approach geared to the development of more effective interpersonal skills on the part of supervisors. The approach is based on the behavioral-learning activities of modeling, behavioral rehearsal, and social reinforcement. The training is structured to maximize the transfer of training from the classroom to the work situation.

Holloway, W.D. Supervisors positive to Interaction Management training. *Assessment & Development*, 1976, *3*(2), 2-6.

This article briefly discusses a study that was conducted at one office of the Massachusetts Mutual Life Insurance Company to evaluate participants' reactions to a recently completed Interaction Management System program. The results indicated that participants viewed the program favorably and perceived the training as a positive, useful experience.

Imitating models: A new management tool. *Business Week*, May 8, 1978, pp. 119-120.

This article describes the growing acceptance of behavior modeling as a training method, the modeling programs that are available, and the success of these programs in various organizations.

Interaction modeling improves supervisory skills. *Behavioral Sciences Newsletter*, May 24, 1976, pp. 1-2.

This article provides a positive critique of the Interaction Management System and predicts a bright future for it. The author briefly describes the system and then discusses its advantages and disadvantages.

Judt, J.P. An evaluation of first-line supervisor skill training. Unpublished master's thesis, University of Nebraska, 1978.

This thesis examines the implementation and subsequent evaluation of the Interaction Management System in Norden Laboratories, Inc., a Nebraska-based animal-health subsidiary of SmithKline Corporation. In evaluating the Norden supervisors' behavior before and after interaction-management training, two types of measurement were used with both the trained group and control group: (1) presurveys and postsurveys of the supervisors' effectiveness and confidence as rated by the supervisors, their subordinates, and their managers, and (2) evaluation of supervisors' handling of videotaped role-play situations in terms of factors such as leadership or control, problem analysis, problem solving, sensitivity, listening, and overall effectiveness.

King, H.D., & Arlinghaus, C.G. Interaction Management validated in the steel industry. *Assessment & Development*, 1976, *3*(2), 1-2.

This article reports on a recent evaluation study, conducted in a heavy-manufacturing setting at Lukens Steel Company, that indicated that interaction-modeling training is effective in measurably increasing the skill level of front-line foremen in handling critical interactions with employees. The evaluation procedure and the results and implications of the study are discussed.

Kraut, A.I. Developing managerial skills via modeling techniques: Some positive research findings—A symposium. *Personnel Psychology*, 1976, *29*(3), 325-328.

The author compares the four major learning activities of behavior modeling with a traditional management-development training model. He concludes that the behavioral-modeling approach is more effective than is the traditional training approach in changing managerial behavior.

Latham, G.P., & Saari, L.M. Application of social-learning theory to training supervisors through behavioral modeling. *Journal of Applied Psychology*, 1979, *64*(3), 239-246.

This article demonstrates how behavior modeling's integration and use of cognitive, behavioral, and environmental variables in the training of supervisors bring about a relatively permanent and positive change in supervisors' behaviors and abilities to manage their subordinates. Research data obtained through the use of reaction questionnaires, learning-measures tests, behavioral simulations, behavioral-observation scales, and performance-appraisal instruments indicate that supervisors who received behavior-modeling training performed more effectively on the job.

Molloy, W.F. Making role plays pay off in training. *Training*, May 1981, pp. 59-63.

According to this article, many people have had negative experiences in role plays. However, role plays can be positive and effective if the training manager follows several key guidelines, which consist of starting with behavioral objectives, using a positive model, and coaching for a success. They also include managing the feedback after the role play in a manner that maintains the self-esteem of the role player and provides the role player with alternative positive behavior. Custom role plays enable the learners to utilize realistic job settings. The instructor who must fulfill several roles (resource person, coach, and manager of feedback) must keep the discussion focused on the interactive process rather than the role-play content.

Moses, J.L. Behavior modeling for managers. *Human Factors*, 1978, *20*(2), 225-232

The author briefly examines the concept of behavior modeling, traces its development, and describes the methodology used. Research findings documenting the effectiveness of this technique and the implications this has for management training and management development are also discussed.

Moses, J., & Ritchie, D. Supervisory Relationships Training. *Human Resources Development*, 1974, *1*, 1-2.

This article describes AT&T's new Supervisory Relationships Training program, which is designed to help first-level supervisors deal more effectively with contemporary work-force problems. The authors discuss how the learning principles of modeling, behavioral rehearsal, feedback, and transfer of training have been used in this problem-related approach to facilitate transfer of skills from the classroom to the job. They also briefly describe evaluation studies of the program that are now under way in two telephone companies.

Moses, J., & Ritchie, D. Assessment center used to evaluate an interaction modeling program. *Assessment & Development*, 1975, *2*(2), 1-2.

This study indicates that supervisors who were trained via interaction modeling were more effective in resolving problem situations with employees than were supervisors—matched by gender, age, department, length of service, and number of subordinates—who were not trained via interaction modeling.

Moses, J.L., & Ritchie, R.J. Supervisory Relationships Training: A behavioral evaluation of a behavior modeling program. *Personnel Psychology*, 1976, *29*(3), 337-343.

The authors describe how the assessment-center method was used to evaluate AT&T's Supervisory Relationship Training program. Trained supervisors were evaluated as being able to resolve the simulated supervisory problems in a much more effective manner than were the untrained supervisors. The trained group was able to utilize skills specifically learned in the training program as well as to generalize these skills to a novel situation.

Nicholson, J. Interaction Management supervisory training evaluation study. Unpublished study, University of Chicago Hospitals and Clinics, 1979.

This study discusses the implementation and subsequent evaluation of Interaction Management (IM) training at the University of Chicago Hospitals and Clinics. The author measures the extent to which IM training results in more effective on-the-job supervision and achieves results in overall supervisory performance and employee performance. The author also describes the evaluation techniques and instruments used in the study, including structured interviews with supervisors after training, a program-evaluation form completed by all participants at the program's end, patterned interviews with managers, and group audit sessions.

91.6 percent of supervisors intend to use Interaction Management skills. *IM Navigator*, 1979, *3*(1), 1-2; 22-23.

This article gives tabulated survey results of a comprehensive behavior-modeling study conducted by Development Dimensions International. Shown are the actual percentages of supervisors and managers trained in the Interaction Management Program or Management Reinforcement Workshop who intend to use Interaction Management skills on the job, the applicability of IM skills for supervisors, the likelihood of managers using Management Reinforcement skills, and satisfaction with procedures used in the workshops. The article also explains the procedure by which IM instructors can compare the scores of individual supervisors and managers they have trained against norms for the total population of supervisors and managers.

Ooley, R.L. IM receives management support at Brown & Williamson Tobacco Corporation. *IM Navigator*, 1977, *1*(1), 8.

The author briefly describes how the problems of ensuring that the skills would be practiced on the job and obtaining supervisor and manager commitment for the program were initially dealt with when Brown & Williamson began implementing the Interaction Management System.

Petasis, A. Behaviour modelling: It can be an efficient training tool. *People & Profits*, 1977, *4*(11), 6-11; 30. Summary of study appears in *IM Navigator*, 1977, *1*(1), 10-12.

The author reports on the effects of introducing Interaction Management training in a large Rhodesian organization. Focusing on the problems of employee performance, poor employee work habits, and poor employee attendance, pretraining and post-training self-report data from supervisors in an experimental group and a control group were collected regarding the number of times (1) these problems cause concern, (2) supervisors tackle these problems when they occur, (3) supervisors assess the status of these problems as showing "considerable improvement," and (4) supervisors feel "very confident" in handling these problems. The author concludes that even though the data basically reflect the respondents' perceptions, Interaction Management does provide at least one method of changing behavior in a positive direction.

Robinson, J.C. Don't blame managers—They don't know how. *Training Management & Motivation*, Fall 1976, pp. 6; 30-33; 35.

The author suggests that most supervisory-training failures are due to lack of reinforcement back on the job rather than failure to learn in the classroom. The traditional top-down approach to management reinforcement and the reasons why this is not appropriate for situational-skills training are discussed. The author describes how managers can be taught to reinforce specific supervisory skills, using the IM Reinforcement Workshop as an example. The need for both management support and management reinforcement is highlighted.

Robinson, J.C. Letter to editor: A model debate. *Northeast Training News*, June 1980, p. 21.

In response to an article in an earlier issue of the magazine, the author points out that there are no standardized behavior-modeling programs. Instead, in reality, those programs refer to standardized/generic programs that offer a variety of skill modules, modeling displays, real situations for skill practicing, and opportunities for commitment to use skills on the job. The author also indicates that research shows there are no differences in the effectiveness of generic and customized modeling displays. Seven characteristics of an effective behavior-modeling program are listed.

Robinson, J.C. Will behavior modeling survive the '80's? *Training and Development Journal*, 1980, *34*(1), 22-28.

This article explores both the strengths and the shortcomings of behavior modeling and offers training professionals clear-cut guidelines for making sure that behavior modeling's technology is utilized appropriately and effectively. Is behavior modeling a fad or is it a "useful instructional technology" with strengths that will enable it to survive the coming decade? In final answer to this question, the author leaves the training community with the challenge to utilize behavior modeling in a manner that enables it to have a positive and lasting impact.

Robinson, J.C., & Gaines, D.L. Seven questions to ask yourself before using behavior modeling. *Training*, December 1980, pp. 60-69.

The authors maintain that, because of their popularity, behavior-modeling programs may be used inappropriately. They therefore provide a flow chart that contains seven decisions. Each decision pertains to a different characteristic of a behavior-modeling program. By objectively making each decision, the reader can determine whether or not behavior modeling would be appropriate for a given situation. A case study is provided to demonstrate the use of the decision-making flow chart.

Robinson, J.C., & Robinson, L.E. Modeling techniques applied to performance feedback and appraisal. *Training and Development Journal*, 1978, *32*(1), 48-53.

The authors review the shortcomings of present supervisory practices and then describe how the PerforMax System has successfully integrated the four managerial functions of goal setting, day-to-day performance feedback, periodic performance appraisals, and management reinforcement in one complete system that enables supervisors to deal effectively with employee performance on a continuing basis. Major emphasis in PerforMax is placed on building supervisors' and managers' performance feedback and appraisal skills through the use of interaction-modeling techniques.

Robinson, J.C., & Robinson, L.E. How to make sure your supervisors do on-the-job what you taught them in the classroom. *Training*, 1979, *16*(9), 21-26.

The authors suggest that there are specific methods trainers can use in conjunction with their supervisory-training programs to ensure that the skills learned in the classroom are transferred to the job. They describe how conducting needs analyses and gaining management support prior to training, developing skill mastery and building confidence during training, and assuring that supervisors are reinforced for using the new skills back on the job are important factors that increase the amount of skill transfer.

Rosenbaum, B. A new approach to changing supervisory behavior. *Personnel*, 1975, *52*, 37-44.

This article summarizes the principles of supervisory training outlined by Goldstein and Sorcher, namely: modeling, behavioral rehearsal, feedback and reinforcement, and transferring training to the job.

Rosenbaum, B.L. Common misconceptions about behavior modeling and supervisory skill training (SST). *Training and Development Journal*, 1979, *33*(8), 40-44.

To help correct common misconceptions surrounding behavior modeling and supervisory-skills training (SST), the article highlights the general principles that learners of behavior modeling and SST are expected to achieve and provides an application of SST in a "model" situation. Refuted in the article are statements such as "Behavior modeling and SST are soft management, phony, manipulative and sneaky, and time-consuming."

Rosenbaum, B.L. Issues and answers. *Northeast Training News*, July 1980, p. 7.

In response to an earlier letter by James Robinson to the *Northeast Training News*, the author maintains that customized modeling displays are more credible than off-the-shelf models. Customizing enables an organization to address issues that are unique to it. The author concurs with the seven factors listed by Robinson as necessary for an effective behavior-modeling program.

Rosenbaum, B.L. New uses for behavior modeling. *Personnel Administrator*, 1978, *23*(7), 27-28.

This article provides a brief description of the behavior-modeling training technique and its application in increasingly diverse situations.

Rosenbaum, B. The modeled supervisor. *Northeast Training News*, March 1980, p. 21.

This article discusses why behavior modeling succeeds where other supervisory-skills-training programs fail, and it gives an explanation of how one company effectively used behavior modeling. Also explored is the reason why custom-designed behavior-modeling programs are more effective than standardized programs. To illustrate this point, the major components of a custom-designed behavior-modeling program are explained and justified.

Smith, P.E. Management modeling training to improve morale and customer satisfaction. *Personnel Psychology*, 1976, *29*(3), 351-359.

This paper focuses on the effect of behavior-modeling training on employee morale, customer satisfaction, and sales. In two studies conducted at IBM, modeling training was effective in improving employee morale, managers' communication skills, and sales performance. In addition, managers who showed greater improvement in their communication skills also showed higher customer satisfaction in their branch offices.

Sorcher, M.A. A behavior modification approach to supervisor training. *Professional Psychology*, 1971, *2*, 401-402.

The potential of behavior-modification techniques in industry is discussed. Emphasis is on increasing the behavioral repertoire of managers by providing them with more adaptive behaviors in a variety of job-relevant situations.

Sorcher, M.A. Behaviour modelling: A new approach to supervisory training. *People & Profits*, 1975, *2*(12), 26-29.

The author describes the concept of behavior modeling and outlines how this technique of teaching interpersonal skills differs from traditional supervisory programs. Emphasis is on behavior change and transfer of training.

Sorcher, M.A. Behaviour modelling: A new approach to supervisory training. *People & Profits*, 1975, *3*(1), 22-29.

The author describes the development of specific behavioral guidelines ("learning points") and discusses why they work. He also demonstrates their use in actual role plays.

Sorcher, M.A. Behaviour modelling: A new approach to supervisory training. *People & Profits*, 1975, *3*(2), 26-30.

Actual research results of behavior-modeling programs, i.e., effect on employee turnover, employee performance, and problem solving, are detailed in this article. The author also discusses current research into the behavior-modeling technique and offers advice on how to develop training programs.

Sorcher, M., & Goldstein, A.P. A behavior modeling approach in training. *Personnel Administration*, 1972, *35*(2), 35-41.

This article outlines the approach taken by the authors for changing supervisory behavior, which they described more fully in their book, *Changing Supervisor Behavior* (see Goldstein & Sorcher, 1974).

Tosti, D.T. Behavior modeling: A process. *Training and Development Journal*, 1980, *34*(8), 70-74.

This article discusses the confusion between the method of behavior modeling and the ways in which it can be utilized. It explains that criticisms of the behavior-modeling method are often really complaints about inappropriate uses of the method. To illustrate this, the article refutes some common misconceptions about behavior modeling, including that it is manipulative and is a system for enhancing self-esteem. In addition, the article explores the major steps in designing an effective behavior-modeling program and the primary errors typically committed in these areas.

Waltz, D. What IM has done and is doing. *IM Navigator*, 1981, *5*(1), 17-18.

The author reports that in DuPont's Sabine River Works, supervisors feel good about how they handle on-the-job interactions with their employees since being trained in Interaction Management. Supervisors report that the single most important factor for their success is the use of the key principle "Maintain or enhance self-esteem." Other factors contributing to the success of the program are top-management support and selection and training of highly competent instructors. Ninety-seven percent of the supervisors were satisfied with the behavior-modeling workshop; 95 percent of the managers felt their subordinate supervisors could use the skills on the job; and 100 percent of the managers felt that the IM skills were applicable to their organization and that they, the managers, would use the management-reinforcement skills on the job.

Wehrenberg, S., & Kuhnle, R. How training through behavior modeling works. *Personnel Journal*, 1980, *59*(7), 576-581.

This article briefly explains the fundamental theory on which behavior modeling is based. The authors also explain the components of a typical behavior-modeling training program and how behavior-modeling training is implemented in an organization. In addition, the article discusses various methods and instruments used to evaluate the impact of behavior-modeling training.

What your trainees can learn by simply watching others. *Training*, 1978, *15*(6), 22-23.

This article briefly describes some of the early modeling research conducted by Miller and Dollard and Albert Bandura. Four processes involved in modeling—attention, retention, reproduction, and reinforcement/motivation—are discussed, as well as various modeling applications.

Wilson, J. Behaviour modelling: A new approach to supervisory training. *People & Profits*, 1975, *3*(4), 24-28.

This article reports on the Interaction Management Supervisory Training Programme currently in use at Rank Xerox (South Africa). The author discusses the results of the program with both white and nonwhite supervisors and cites many enthusiastic and positive responses. He also describes the approach used within the company and the levels of supervision involved.

Zemke, R. Behavior modeling: Using the "monkey see, monkey do" principle in training. *Training*, 1978, *15*(6), 21-26.

The article explores the theory behind behavior-modeling programs and why behavior modeling is successful. In addition, the author cites several evaluations of successful behavior-modeling programs.

Zemke, R. Building behavior models that work. *Training*, 1982, *19*(1), 22-27.

This article reviews the state of the art on developing modeling displays, and states that experts seem to agree on the major guidelines but that designing them is still an art with the particulars open to disagreement. The discussions and interviews with various experts center around four main issues to consider when developing and evaluating modeling displays: dressing the set, perfect versus coping performance, real versus neutral content, and negative versus positive examples.

Acknowledgements

Many people have contributed to the thoughts and examples in this book. These people include my colleagues, clients, and friends. Unfortunately, I cannot mention every person in this section, but I would like to acknowledge a few personally.

The work of Mel Sorcher and Arnie Goldstein was the genesis of this book. Mel and Arnie did the first work in behavior modeling with supervisors. They also introduced me to behavior modeling and showed me its great potential.

Paul Steiger of Agway Inc. worked with me on the first implementation of behavior modeling at Agway. Together we brought a behavior-modeling program for supervisory training to the eighteen supervisors in Agway's three distribution centers in the early Seventies.

Ann Kiggins and Diane Adams worked with me at Agway during the early days of behavior modeling. They helped me to expand the behavior-modeling program—from the distribution centers to, eventually, many other groups of supervisors in that organization. Ann and Diane implemented and completed the evaluation study with the Agway accounting-department managers.

Bill Byham of Development Dimensions International (DDI) and Doug Bray of American Telephone & Telegraph saw the great potential of behavior modeling and encouraged me to design the first generic behavior-modeling program, which was later used by many different organizations. That program, however, could not have been completed without Linda Robinson, who expertly handled many jobs, including those of program developer, assistant film director, secretary, editor, and jack-of-all-trades.

My colleagues in DDI have continually given me insight, feedback, and encouragement. Many of the case studies in this book are drawn from situations in which DDI consultants have been involved. I particularly want to note the suggestions and feedback provided me by Ken Hofmeister, Judy McCastle, Danny Hupp, Barbara Kelly, Gary Haverland, Linn Coffman, and Ken Hultman.

There is no way that all the parts of this book would have come together without Barbara Mazur, my administrative assistant. She has coordinated input from many people and in some magical way has been able to align all the pieces of the book into a logical sequence.

Special thanks is given for the support of the DDI staff, particularly those dedicated people in word processing under the direction of Jane Lindt and in DDI's publications department under the direction of Dennis McKee. Particular thanks are owed to Bill Proudfoot and Ric Anthony, who spent hours editing some very rough copy.

A special word of thanks goes to Leslie Stephen, managing editor of Learning Concepts. Leslie has provided encouragement, feedback, guidance, and support. She was truly outstanding in her ability to clarify my sometimes inarticulate thoughts. Her support encouraged me to continue with the book even when the task seemed overwhelming. I can truly say that without Leslie this book would not have been written.

About the Author

Since 1972, Jim Robinson has been involved in behavior modeling. That year, he conducted his first behavior-modeling workshop with six Agway Inc. distribution-center supervisors.

Since then, he has developed the Interaction Management System, which offers over fifty modules for supervisory development, and has pioneered the use of management-reinforcement and competency-based instructor workshops to accompany behavior-modeling programs. He has written numerous articles on supervisory development, behavior modeling, and skill transfer. His consulting and speaking engagements have taken him to Japan, Brazil, Africa, Canada, and throughout the United States.

Jim Robinson has looked at management development from several vantage points—as a line manager in Agway, as the training director of Agway, and now as an executive at Development Dimensions International, with responsibility for its supervisory-development programs.